CHRISTIANITY
or the CHURCH?

By Archbishop Ilarion (Troitsky)

Translated by Holy Trinity Monastery

HOLY TRINITY PUBLICATIONS
The Printshop of St Job of Pochaev
Holy Trinity Monastery
Jordanville, New York
2024

Printed with the blessing of His Grace,
Bishop Luke of Syracuse
and Abbot of Holy Trinity Monastery

original text © 1971, 1977 Holy Trinity Monastery
Revisions and added material: Christianity or the Church?
© 2024 Holy Trinity Monastery

PRINTSHOP OF
SAINT JOB OF POCHAEV

An imprint of

HOLY TRINITY PUBLICATIONS
Holy Trinity Monastery
Jordanville, New York 13361-0036
www.holytrinitypublications.com

ISBN: 978-0-88465-496-4 (paperback)
ISBN: 978-0-88465-512-1 (ePub)

Library of Congress Control Number: 2024940340

Cover: Image: "The Kremlin in Moscow," Postcard, circa 1910, Source:
dreamstime.com: ID 23785093. © Gors4730.

New Testament Scripture passages taken from the New King James Version.
Copyright © 1982 by Thomas Nelson, Inc. Used by permission.
Psalms taken from A Psalter for Prayer, trans. David James
(Jordanville, N.Y.: Holy Trinity Publications, 2011).
Old Testament and Apocryphal passages taken from the Orthodox Study Bible.
Copyright © 2008 by Thomas Nelson, Inc. Used by permission.

This translation is dedicated to the memory of the Holy New Martyrs of the Solovetsky Monastery, that monastery which in former days witnessed the prayerful spiritual and physical struggles of God-seeking monks, and in latter times received the blood of Holy Martyrs, not the least of whom is Archbishop Ilarion (Troitsky).

Contents

Preface

This short but vital work was composed in Russian at the beginning of the twentieth century, just before the horrors of the First World War and the Bolshevik Revolution were unleashed upon the Russian Empire and its peoples. As these words were written, efforts were already underway amongst Protestants to create some kind of unified ecclesial reality that would ultimately lead to the creation of the body known as the "World Council of Churches" that still exists to our own time.

Such human efforts have failed to produce an alternative to the salvific reality of the one Church of Christ that we confess is already and only to be found in the One Holy Catholic and Apostolic Church of Christ that is the Orthodox Church. Archbishop Saint Ilarion was a preeminent teacher of the dogma of the Church and this short work amply conveys a succinct summary of his teaching: No authentic Christian religion can be found that is separated from the life of the Church.

More than a century after he penned these words, their message needs to be heard and heeded. As Western culture continues to secularize and as "Truth," is relativized and given no objective meaning, this work remains a gold standard for those seeking to obey the words of Jesus: "Take heed that no one deceives you. For many will come in My name, saying, 'I am He,' and will deceive many" (Mark 13:5–6).

Holy Trinity Monastery

 **Introduction**

Usually, people prefer to remain silent concerning a matter which they know nothing about and do not understand. This, of course, is completely sensible. Let us imagine, for example, a person who knows nothing about chemistry but who, nevertheless, constantly insists upon interfering in the affairs of chemists. He corrects their scientific formulae which have been obtained with great difficulty, changing their order or replacing one with another. We would agree that such a person is acting with the highest degree of imprudence and that we can only have pity for him.

There is one field, however, in which too many people consider themselves to be complete masters, in fact, almost legislators; that is the area concerning the Christian faith and the Church. In this field also, clear and definite formulae have been established with a great effort of theological thought, spiritual guidance, faith, and piety. These formulae are established and must be accepted on faith. Regardless of this fact, a great many people enter into the questions of faith and the Church solely as bold and decisive reformers who want to remake everything according to their own personal desires. In cases where such people have insufficient knowledge or understanding, they are especially averse to remaining silent. On the contrary they begin not only to speak, but to shout. Such shouting on the questions of faith and the Church usually fills the columns of newspapers and the ordinary conversations of people who, in general, very seldom think of faith and the Church at all. If they do think of such things, they prefer to voice themselves exclusively in an authoritative and accusatory tone.

In such an atmosphere a great multitude of various perverse opinions are born which then become fashionable because no one will trouble himself to consider and examine them. In the prevalence of such opinions, it can easily occur that they are unconsciously assimilated even by people who are dedicated in their souls to the faith and the Church.

One of the greatest of these prevalent and "accepted" opinions is what we would call "the separation of Christianity from the Church." We would like to examine it with the help of the word of God and the writings of the holy Fathers.

PART I

The Unity of Believers

The life of Christ the Saviour presents the reader of the Holy Gospels with numerous great moments which fill the soul with some special sense of grandeur. But perhaps the greatest moment in the life of all mankind was that occasion when, in the darkness of a southern night, under the hanging arches of trees just turning green, through which heaven itself seemed to be looking at the sinful earth with twinkling stars, the Lord Jesus Christ, in His High Priestly prayer, proclaimed:

> Holy Father, keep through Your name those whom You have given Me, that they may be one as We are. . . . I do not pray for these alone, but also for those who will believe in Me through their word; that they all may be one, as You, Father, are in Me, and I in You; that they also may be one in Us, that the world may believe that You sent Me. (John 17:11; 20–21)

Special attention must be focused upon these words of Christ, for in them the essence of all Christianity is clearly defined. Christianity is not some sort of abstract teaching which is accepted by the mind and *found by each person separately*. On the contrary, Christianity is a life in which separate persons are so united among themselves that their unity can be likened to the unity of the Persons of the Holy Trinity. Christ did not pray only that His teaching be preserved so that it would spread throughout the universe. He prayed for the unification of all those believing in Him. Christ prayed to His heavenly Father for the establishment, more correctly for the restoration, on earth of the natural unity of all mankind. Mankind was created from one common origin and of one source (cf. Acts 17:26).

According to the words of Saint Basil the Great, "Mankind would not have had divisions, nor discord, nor wars if sin had not divided his nature," and "this is the main point of God's saving economy of His incarnation—to bring human nature into unity with Himself and with the Saviour. Then, having destroyed the evil part, to re-establish the original unity as the finest physician, through curative treatment, again mends the body which had been cut up in pieces."[1] The Church is formed of this unification of individuals; not of the apostles only, but of all those who believe in Christ according to their words. No earthly thing has ever been found which could be compared to the new community of saved people. There is no form of unity on earth with which one could compare the unity that is the

Church. Such unity was found only in heaven. In heaven, the incomparable love of the Father, the Son, and the Holy Spirit unites three Persons into one Being so that there are not three Beings, but One God living a triune life. Those people about whom Christ prayed to the heavenly Father: "that the love with which You loved Me may be in them, and I in them" (John 17:26) are also called to such a love which could fuse many into a state of one-ness.

In the aforementioned words of Christ, the truth of the Church is placed into the tightest union with the mystery of the All-holy Trinity. People who enter the Church and love Her become like the three Persons of the Holy Trinity, whose love unites them into one being. The Church is like a one-essence of many persons, created by the moral beginning of love. This is precisely the theme which is perceived in the first sacred prayer of Christ the Saviour by very many of the eminent Fathers and teachers of the Church: Saints Cyprian of Carthage, Basil the Great, Gregory of Nyssa, Ambrose of Milan, Hilary of Poitiers, Cyril of Alexandria, Augustine of Hippo, and John Cassian. Allow me to introduce short excerpts on this subject from the writings of some of this great and renowned assembly of Fathers.

Saint Cyprian of Carthage, in his letter to Magnus, says: "The Lord, teaching us that unity comes from divine authority, affirms and says: 'I and My Father are one' (John 10:30; cf. John 10:16)."[2] In his composition "The

Lord's Prayer," Cyprian also says: "Not being satisfied that
He expiated us by His blood, He also interceded for us.
While interceding for us, here is what He desired: that we
will live in the very same state of unity in which the Father
and the Son are one."[3]

Here is what Saint Cyril of Alexandria writes: "Christ,
having taken as an example and image of that indivisible
love, accord and unity which is conceivable only in unanimity, the unity of essence which the Father has with
Him and which He, in turn, has with His Father, desires
that we too should unite with each other; evidently in the
same way as the consubstantial Holy Trinity is united so
that the whole body of the Church is conceived of as one,
ascending in Christ through the fusion and union of two
people into the composition of the new perfect whole.
The image of Divine unity and the consubstantial nature
of the Holy Trinity as a most perfect interpenetration
must be reflected in the unity of the believers who are of
one heart and mind." Saint Cyril also points out "the natural unity by which we are all bound together, and all of us
to God, cannot exist without bodily unity."[4]

All the earthly works of Christ, therefore, must not
be thought of as teaching alone. Christ did not come
to earth to announce some novel theoretical propositions to mankind. No! He came in order to create a
completely new life for mankind, that is, the Church.
Christ Himself said that He would build the Church: "I

will build My church, and the gates of Hades shall not prevail against it" (Matt 16:18).

This new human community, according to the conception of the Creator Himself, differs vitally from all other associations of people into various societies. Christ Himself often referred to His Church as the Kingdom of God and said that this Kingdom is not of the world, that is, its nature is not of the world, not temporal; it is not comparable with earthly kingdoms. "My peace I give to you; not as the world gives do I give to you" (John 14:27). "My kingdom is not of this world. If My kingdom were of this world, My servants would fight, so that I should not be delivered to the Jews; but now My kingdom is not from here" (John 18:36; cf. John 15:19; 17:16; 17:14–16).

New Testament Teaching and the Church

The idea of the Church as a new, perfect community as distinct from a community of the state organization is profoundly and beautifully expressed in the kontakion for Pentecost Sunday, the feast of the descent of the Holy Spirit, when the Church recalls and celebrates its beginning. "Once, when He descended and confounded the tongues, the Most High divided the nations; and when He divided the tongues of fire, He called all men into unity; and with one accord we glorify the All-Holy Spirit."[5] Here the creation of the Church is placed into opposition to the Tower of Babel and the *confusing of tongues*, at which time

God, the Most High, came down, confused the tongues, and divided the nations.

The biblical narrative of the Tower of Babel has an extremely profound meaning. It is just before this event that the Bible relates the first successes of sinful mankind in the areas of culture and society. It was at this time that man began to build stone cities. At this point the Lord confused the languages of those living on earth so that they stopped understanding each other and were scattered over the entire earth (cf. Gen 11:5–9). In this "Babylonian tower building" we are presented with a certain general type of civil or state society based on an externally legal norm.

The Russian philosopher Vladimir S. Solovyov defined law thus: "Law is a compulsory demand for the realization of a certain minimum of good or order which does not allow certain manifestations of evil."[6] Even if we accepted this definition of law, it is evident that it would never correspond to Christian morals. Law touches the external aspect and by-passes the essence of man. A society created on a legal basis can never merge people into unity. Unity is destroyed through self-love and egoism, for law does not destroy egoism. On the contrary, law only affirms it, guarding it from an encroachment on the part of the egoism of others. The purpose of a state based on law consists of creating, as far as possible, such an order in which the egoism of each member can find satisfaction for itself without violating the interests of others. The only path to the creation of such an order can be to place a certain limitation on the egoism of individual members. In this we have the unsolvable contradiction of law: it affirms egoism, yet it imposes limitations upon it. Therefore, a society formed on a legal basis always carries within itself the seeds of its own decay, for it guards egoism which constantly corrodes all unity. The fate of the tower of Babylon is the fate of legal society. In such a society there must frequently occur a "confusion of tongues" when people stop understanding each other even though they speak the same language. Legal order often gives place to terrible disorder.

The Christian society—the Church—is in direct contrast to such a legal, purely temporal society. But when "He divided the tongues of fire, He called all men into unity."[7] Christ did not create the Church as a means of guarding human egoism, but as a means of its complete destruction.

The basis of Church unity does not consist of legal principles, which guard personal egoism, but love, which is the opposite of personal egoism. In His parting conversation, Christ said to His disciples: "A new commandment I give to you, that you love one another; as I have loved you, that you also love one another. By this all will know that you are My disciples, if you have love for one another" (John 13:34–35).

It is this *new beginning* of Church unity which creates an organic unity rather than a mechanical unification of internally divided persons. Christ Himself likened Church unity to the organic unity of a tree with its branches (cf. Rom 11:16–24).

The Apostle Paul spoke in great detail concerning the organic unity of the Church. He also compared the Church to a tree, but more often, the Apostle Paul refers to the Church as a "body" (σώμα). "For as we have many members in one body, but all the members do not have the same function, so we, being many, are one body in Christ, and individually members of one another" (Rom 12:4–5).[8] Referring to the Church as a body immediately implies its unity, for two bodies cannot be organically joined to one another. This term also indicates the special character of the unification of the members who enter into the composition of the Church. The image of the body in application to the Church is beautifully revealed by the Apostle Paul. All who enter in the Church are members separately, but together comprise one body in Christ (cf. 1 Cor 12:20). The body is one, but it has many members and all are members of one body; although they be many, they compose one body. The body is not composed of one member, but of many. If the leg says, "I do not belong to the body because I am not an arm," does it then in actual fact not belong to the body? And if the ear will say, "I do not belong to the body because I am not an eye," does it then not belong to the body?

God arranged each of the members of the body as it was pleasing to Him (cf. 1 Cor 11:12; 12:24). Just as we have many members in one body, not all members have the same function. The eye cannot say to the hand, "I have no need of you." nor can the head say such a thing to the legs. God proportioned the body of mutually interdependent parts, but all members are equally responsive to one another. Thus, if one member suffers, all the members suffer with it; if one of the members becomes great, all the members rejoice with it (1 Cor 12:21). "God composed the body, having given greater honor to that part which lacks it, that there should be no schism in the body, but that the members should have the same care for one another. And if one member suffers, all the members suffer with it; or if one member is honored, all the members rejoice with it" (1 Cor 12:24–26; cf. Rom 12:6–9).

But how is it possible to implement such a unity of people in a Church community? The natural state of man corresponds more to the creation of a merely legal society, for sin is the self-assertion and self-love which is guarded by civil law. Indeed, as long as man guards his sinful state, complete unity will be an empty dream which cannot be brought to reality.

Such an implementation is, however, made possible by the concept of the Church. Christ gave the commandment to love one another, but the commandment alone is insufficient. Like every theoretical proposition, it can create nothing if the power for the fulfillment is not provided. If Christianity limited itself to the theoretical teaching of love, it would be of no use because the power for the realization of this teaching is not available in human nature, which is distorted by sin. Reason confesses that this commandment about love is good, but man constantly meets a different law within himself which struggles against the law of the mind and which makes him captive to the sinful law. "For I delight in the law of God according to the inward man. But I see another law in my members, warring against the law of my mind, and bringing me into captivity to the law of sin which is in my members" (Rom 7:22–23). The work of Christ, however, is not limited to theoretical propositions and it is in this that the strength and significance of His work rests.

Mankind is given new strength and so the new unity of the Church is possible for him. There is a new beginning, a new source of life—the Holy Spirit. Christ Himself said that he who is not born of water and of the Spirit cannot enter into the Kingdom of God:

"Most assuredly, I say to you, unless one is born again, he cannot see the kingdom of God." Nicodemus said to Him [Jesus], "How can a man be born when he is old? Can he enter a second time into his mother's womb and be born?"... Jesus answered, "Most assuredly, I say to you, unless one is born of water and the Spirit, he cannot enter the kingdom of God. That which is born of the flesh is flesh, and that which is born of the Spirit is spirit. Do not marvel that I said to you, 'You must be born again.' The wind blows where it wishes, and you hear the sound of it, but cannot tell where it comes from and where it goes. So is everyone who is born of the Spirit." (John 3:3–8)

It is necessary to be born of the Spirit. When the Apostle Paul speaks about the unity of people in the Church, he always speaks of the Holy Spirit as the source of this unity.

For the Apostle Paul, the Church is not only a single body, but also *a single Spirit*: "But one and the same Spirit works all these things, distributing to each one individually as He wills. . . . For by one Spirit we were all baptized into one body—whether Jews or Greeks, whether slaves or free—and have all been made to drink into one Spirit" (1 Cor 12:11, 13; cf. Eph 4:3–6). Here we understand, not a conformity of ideas or a unity of religious convictions, as certain Western thinkers wish to believe, but a single Spirit of God which penetrates the entire body of the Church, as the holy Fathers and teachers of the Church testify.

"What is the unity of the Spirit?" asks Saint John Chrysostom, and he answers, "Just as the spirit, in the body, controls all and communicates some sort of unity to the diversity which arises from the various bodily members, so it is here. But the Spirit is also given in order to unite people who are diverse among themselves in descent and in their way of thinking."[9] "With these words [a single Spirit] he [the Apostle Paul] desired to implant in them a mutual accord, as if saying: 'since you received one Spirit and drank from one Source, then there must be no discord among you.'"[10]

Blessed Theodoret says, "You are all considered worthy of a common Spirit; you compose one body."[11] Blessed Jerome describes: "One body in the sense of the body of Christ, which is the Church; and one Holy Spirit, one single dispenser and sanctifier of all."[12] Blessed Theophylact of Ochrid wrote: "Just as the spirit in the body is the foundation which binds and unites all, though the members are diverse, so the Holy Spirit dwelling in the believers unites all even though they differ from one another by birth, temperament, and pursuits."[13]

According to the teaching of the Apostle Paul, all Church life is a manifestation of God's Holy Spirit; each manifestation of love, each virtue is the action of a gift of the Spirit. According to the words of the Apostle Peter, people are but stewards of the manifold grace of God (cf. 1 Pet 4:10). The Spirit of God has, by His own power, penetrated the entire body of the Church and given various spiritual gifts to each of its members, making possible a new life for mankind. It unites all into one body, unifying in such a way as to instill a kind of love in the hearts of men which, in their natural state, cannot be a principle of their lives and relationships with other people.

Love is of God—this dictum of the Apostle John. "Whoever keeps His word, truly the love of God is perfected in him. By this we know that we are in Him" (1 John 2:5: cf. 1 John 4:9; 3:17). "Love is of God" can be termed as the general theme of a whole series of apostolic discourses. Love is given the title of God. The love of Christ constrains the members of the Church: "for the love of Christ compels us ..." (2 Cor 5:14). Love is the fruit of the Spirit (cf. Gal 5:22). God's love is poured out into our hearts by the Holy Spirit, which is given to us (cf. Rom 5:5). God saved us by means of the renewing action of the Holy Spirit which He shed freely upon us through Jesus Christ our Saviour (cf. Tit 3:5–6).

Thus, the Holy Spirit Who dwells in the Church gives each member of the Church strength to become a new creature whose life is guided by love. The teaching of the Apostle Paul concerning the Church is inseparably linked with his teaching of love as the fundamental principle of Christian life. This connection is little noticed by contemporary scholarly commentators, but the holy Fathers of the Church point it out. Concerning this apostolic comparison of the Church with the body, Blessed Theodoret says, "this comparison is appropriate in the teaching of love."[14] Saint John Chrysostom, interpreting the words, a single body, says, "Paul demands from us a love that would bind us together, making us inseparable one from another, and of such complete unity that we seem to be members of one body. Only such a love as this produces great good."[15]

In reading the epistles of the Apostle Paul, one may note that he usually speaks about the Church and about love side by side. This, of course, is because both of these ideas are inseparably linked together in the very system of the apostle. All of his Christian ethics are based upon the dogmatic teaching about the Church. Thus, in the last chapters of his epistle to the Romans, the apostle speaks in detail about Christian morals. "Let love be without hypocrisy. Abhor what is evil. Cling to what is good. Be kindly affectionate to one another with brotherly love" (Rom 12:9–10). This discourse begins with the ninth verse of the twelfth chapter, and in the five preceding verses (4–8), as the apostle briefly sets forth the teaching of the Church as a body. In the first Epistle to the Corinthians, the teaching about the Church in the twelfth chapter is directly followed by his teaching on love "...but the greatest of these is love" (1 Cor 13:1–13). Something similar to this can also be noted in the epistles to the Ephesians and the Colossians.

What follows from all that has been said? The teaching of Christ is a teaching not only about the re-creation of a separate moral person, but also about the re-creation of a perfect society, that is about the Church. God's Spirit, living in the Church, gives strength for the realization of Christian teaching in life. Since this teaching is a teaching about love, then its realization again creates a community because love is a foundation which binds and does not divide.

Outside the Church and without the Church, Christian life is impossible. Without the Church, the Christian teaching alone remains as an empty sound, for Christian life is Church life. *Only in the life of the Church can a person live and develop.* In a bodily organism, separate members never grow or develop independently of one another, but always and only in connection with the whole organism. The same applies to the Church. For the growth of the Church is at the same time the growth of its members.

In the New Testament writings, the purpose of the existence of the Church is revealed as the moral perfection of human nature. According to the Apostle Paul, spiritual gifts and all services in general exist in the Church for the fulfillment of the saints, that is for the moral re-birth of Christians until we all come to one-ness in our faith and in our comprehension of the knowledge of the Son of God, becoming the perfect man, mature with the fullness of Christ (cf. Eph 4:13).

That is why the Apostle depicts that process by which the reborn mankind reaches the full maturity of Christ. By "speaking the truth in love, may grow up in all things into Him who is the head—Christ—from whom the whole body, joined and knit together by what every joint supplies, according to the effective working by which every part does its share, causes growth of the body for the edifying of itself in love" (Eph 4:15–16). Without entering into a detailed analysis of the Greek text,[16] we will confine ourselves to explaining the thought which the apostle is expressing.[17]

The whole body of the Church is united in a steadily increasing harmony by means of the perception of the abundant gifts of the Holy Spirit which act in each member in a special way. Thus the body of the Church reaches perfection in all its members. All the growth of the entire Church organism depends on each separate member sacredly observing the law of love. The perception of the gift of the Spirit is possible only through love and in union with the Church.

This is the way the aforementioned words of the holy apostle are understood by Saint John Chrysostom,[18] Blessed Theodoret,[19] Saint John of Damascus,[20] and Blessed Theophylact.[21] Their thoughts are brought together by Saint Theophan the Recluse whose words we cite: "Christian faith joins the faithful with Christ and thus it composes one harmonious body from separate individuals. Christ fashions this body by communicating Himself to each member and by supplying to them the Spirit of Grace in an effectual, tangible manner. Thus, the Spirit of Grace descending on each makes him what he ought to be in the body of Christ's Church. Christ's body being harmoniously fit together through this gift of the Spirit, builds itself up in proportion to the measure in which each member answers his purpose or acts for the welfare of the Church in all the fullness of the gift of Grace received."[22]

From this teaching of the Apostle Paul and the interpretation of it by the holy Fathers quoted above, it is evident that, according to the New Testament, the perfection of the human personality depends upon its belonging to the Church as a living organism, undergoing growth through the beneficial and abundant influence of the Holy Spirit. If the bond with the body of the Church becomes severed then the personality which is thereby isolated and enclosed in its own egoism will be deprived of the beneficial and abundant influence of the Holy Spirit which dwells in the Church.

"As a matter of fact, if it happened that the hand became separated from the body, the spirit coming from the brain, seeking continued connection and not finding it there, would not break loose from the body and pass over into the severed hand. If the hand is not there, it no longer receives any communication. The same applies here if we are no longer bound together by love."[23] "All that has separated from the vital source cannot—with the loss of the saving essence—live and breathe with a special life."[24] "Take the sun's ray away from its source—its unity will not permit it to exist as a separate light. Break off a branch from a tree—the broken part will lose the ability to grow. Separate a stream from its source—the separated part will dry up. Likewise, the Church, illuminated by the Lord's light, spreads its rays over all the world; but the light which pours out everywhere is one, and the unity of the body remains undivided. It extends its boughs, heavy with fruit, over all the earth; its abundant streams flow far; and always, the Head remains One. One beginning, one mother, rich with ripening fruitfulness."[25]

In these animated and poetic words, the idea is clearly conveyed that a separate individual or even a separate Christian community is alive only insofar as it lives Christ's life, insofar as it is unified with the Universal Church. To remain aloof or to be locked up in one's self places the individual or even the local church in the same position as a ray separated from the sun, a stream from the source, or a branch from the trunk of the tree. Spiritual life can exist only in an organic unity with the Universal Church; if this unity is broken, then Christian life will dry up.

We hope that it has been made sufficiently clear that the concept of the Church has a paramount significance in the teaching of the New Testament.

Christianity is not concerned with the interests of reason, but only with those of the salvation of man. In Christianity, therefore, there are no purely theoretical tenets. Dogmatic truths have moral significance, and Christian morals are founded on dogma. Included in the concept of the Church is this: the Church is that point at which dogma becomes moral teaching and Christian dogmatics become Christian life. The Church thus comprehended gives life to and provides for the implementation of Christian teaching. Without the Church there is no Christianity; there is only the Christian teaching which, by itself, cannot "renew the fallen Adam," cannot renew creation from its fallen state.

The Early Christian Community

If we now turn from the doctrine of the Church as revealed in the New Testament to the facts of the history of Christianity, we shall see that this is precisely the concept which was fundamental to the Christian view and which had been shaping its reality. Before anything else, the Christians became conscious of themselves as members of the Church. The Christian community referred to itself as a "Church" in preference to all other names. The word "Church" (ἐκκλησία / *ekklesia*) appears one hundred and ten times in the New Testament, while such words as "Christianity" and similar words with the same ending[26] are completely unknown in the New Testament. After the descent of the Holy Spirit on Christ's disciples and apostles, the Church came into being as a visible community with a spiritual interrelation among its members.

At first there was no comprehensive system of teaching. The faith of Christ was set down in a few of the general dogmas. There was nothing to be learned in Christianity and little common accord called for in any abstract propositions. What did it mean at that time to be a Christian?

In our times we hear many various answers, such as to be a Christian means to recognize Christ's teaching, to try to fulfill His commandments. This, of course, is the best of such answers. The first Christians, however, answered the question in a completely different way. From the very first pages of its history, Christianity appears before us in the form of a harmonious and unanimous community. Outside of this community there were no Christians. To come to believe in Christ, to become a Christian—this meant uniting with the Church. This is repeatedly expressed in the book of the Acts of the Apostles, where we read that "the Lord added to the church daily those who were being saved" (Acts 2:47; cf. 5:14). Each new believer was like a branch grafted to the tree of Church life.

Here is a more distinctive example, an illustration of precisely this joining to the Church. The persecutor Saul who had breathed threatening and murderous desires against the Lord's disciples, underwent a miraculous conversion on the road to Damascus, and became a follower of Christ. Here before us is a special revelation of God to man. In Damascus, the Lord sent Ananias to baptize Saul. Saul then traveled to Jerusalem in order to join himself to the disciples there. After Barnabas had informed the Apostles about him, he abode as one among them (Acts 9:27–30). Thus, even the future great Apostle whom, in the vision of Ananias, the Lord calls a chosen instrument (Acts 9:12–15), immediately after conversion became united with the Church which was a visible community. Here is graphic evidence that the Lord does not want to know His servants outside of the Church.[27]

It is easy to understand why the holy Apostle Paul speaks so persistently about the Church in his epistles: he is not creating a teaching about the Church, for during his very conversion Paul knew precisely this Church and not something else, for he recalls subsequently: "For you have heard of my former conduct in Judaism, how I persecuted the church of God beyond measure and tried to destroy it" (Gal 1:13). Saul did not persecute followers of some kind of teaching, but, specifically, the Church, as a defined value, perceivable even to "outsiders."

According to the witness of the compiler of the Acts, the first Christian community was the almost complete realization of this concept of the Church. We read in the Acts of the Apostles that "the multitude of those who believed were of one heart and one soul" (Acts 4:32). It is remarkable that during the fourth century, while the dogma concerning the Holy Trinity was being explained, certain of the holy Fathers used the analogy of the early Christians to describe the unity of the Holy Trinity. How sharply the first Christian community was defined is beautifully demonstrated in one verse from Acts which has somehow been passed over unnoticed. "They were all with one accord in Solomon's Porch. Yet none of the rest dared join them, but the people esteemed them highly" (Acts 5:12–13). Thus, on the one hand, conversion to Christianity is conceived of as uniting with the Church, and on the other hand, "yet none of the rest dared join them." Is it not clear, then, that from the very beginning when the direct disciples of Christ were still alive, Christianity was a visible society—the Church, because the Church was not a theory then; it was life itself.

In the works of Saint Irenaeus of Lyon and Hippolytus of Rome, one learns of the rise of heretical communities which separated from the Church and were referred to as the "School." In the first centuries, the Church was already opposed to the school. It was almost a curse word to the ancient Christians. Using this name, they emphasized their own view that outside the Church there is no Christian life, there is room only for a school of rationalism, for scholastic philosophy.

It is even possible to introduce evidence from outside the Church. It is well known how Protestants have distorted the idea of the Church, preaching a kind of teaching about an "invisible" Church. This teaching is so vague, obscure, and indefinite, that a Lutheran theologian, in an official report at the Diet of Speyer in 1875, declared: "Our Protestant teaching about the Church still distinguishes itself with such vagueness and inconsistency, that it can be called the Achilles' heel of Protestantism."[28] Nevertheless,

Protestants sometimes attempt to attribute their teaching about the Church to early Christianity. Some of the Protestant scholars resolutely declare that the foundations of the visible Church contradict evangelical Christianity and have distorted it. Such, for example, was the point of view of Rudolf Sohm.[29] Lately, however, even in Protestant studies, no such decisive voices are heard concerning the Church of the first centuries. Scholarship alien to the Church is slowly arriving at the realization of the truth that the Church and Christianity were identical concepts and completely inseparable from one another from the very beginning.

Finally, we would make a big omission if we did not cite a few judgments of ancient Church writers on the question interesting us. We shall dwell on the views of two writers who had labored much on the understanding of the dogma of the Church—Saint Cyprian of Carthage and Blessed Augustine.

According to the words of Saint Cyprian, to be a Christian means to belong to the visible Church and to submit to the hierarchy which God has placed in it. The Church is the realization of Christ's love and any separation from the Church is a violation of this love, in which both heretics and schismatics sin equally. This is the basic thought of his treatise "On the Unity of the Catholic Church." This idea is constantly repeated in his letters: "Christ granted us peace; He commanded us to be in harmony and unanimity; He commanded that we preserve, inviolably and firmly, the bond of affection and love. Whoever violates the love of Christ by faithless dissent will no longer belong to Christ: he who does not possess this love does not possess God either. Those who do not desire to be unanimous in God's Church cannot abide with God."[30]

Heretics and schismatics do not have this love, that is the basic Christian virtue and, thus, they are Christian in name only. "Heretics and schismatics preserve neither the unity of the Church nor brotherly love."[31] "They act against the love of Christ."[32] "Marcian who joined with Novatian,[33] became an enemy of charity and love."[34] "It is well known that the heretics have deviated from the love and unity of the universal Church."[35] "What unity is observed, what love is preserved or what love is dreamt about by one who, having given himself up to fits of dissension, leaves the Church, destroys faith, troubles the peace, eradicates love and profanes the sacraments?"[36]

Saint Cyprian even expressed the decisive thought that, not only can there be no Christian life outside the Church, but there can be no Christian teaching either. The pure faith exists only in the Church.[37] Saint Cyprian also calls the Church by the name "Truth,"[38] and teaches that the unity of the faith cannot be separated from the unity of the Church,[39] for truth is one even as the Church is one.[40]

He who does not adhere to the unity of the Church cannot think that he is preserving the faith.[41] Any separation from the Church is, without fail, connected with the distortion of the faith. "The enemy has contrived heresies and schisms in order to overthrow the faith, distort the truth, and dissolve unity. His servants proclaim the treachery under the pretense of faith, herald the antichrist in the name of Christ; and concealing the lie by means of imitating righteousness subtly, they guilefully destroy the truth."[42]

"Just as Satan is not Christ although he deceives in His name, so one cannot be a Christian if he does not abide in the truth of His gospel and faith."[43] A heretic cleaving to this own way divides the Church and destroys faith; … he arms himself against the Church. In relation to the faith, he is a traitor; in relation to piety, he is a defiler, a recalcitrant servant, a lawless son, a hostile brother."[44]

"If one examines the faith of those who believe outside the Church, it would be found that heretics have a completely different faith; as a matter of fact they have only a wild fanaticism, blasphemy, and a decay which is fighting against holiness and truth."[45] According to Saint Cyprian, to be outside the Church and yet remain a Christian is impossible, for to be outside the Church is to be outside Christ's camp.[46]

Those who separate themselves from the Church and those who act against the Church are antichrists and heathens.[47] Here, for example, is what Saint Cyprian writes to Antonius concerning Novatian: "You have desired, most beloved brother, that I write you concerning Novatian, what heresy he has introduced. Know that, first of all, we must not be curious about what he teaches when he is teaching outside the Church. *No matter who or what he is, he is not a Christian as soon as he is not in the Church of Christ* [emphasis added]."[48] "How can anyone be with Christ if he does not dwell within the Bride of Christ, if he is not found in His Church?"[49]

Finally, in the treatise, "On the Unity of the Catholic Church," we read the famous words:

"He who does not have the Church as his mother cannot have God as his Father."[50]

Saint Cyprian completely refuses the name "Christian" to all those who stand outside the Church, as if repeating the decisive exclamation of his teacher Tertullian: "*haeretici christiani esse non possunt!*"—"Heretics cannot be Christians!"

> He who does not have the Church as his mother cannot have God as his Father.

Thus we can understand Saint Cyprian's demand that even Novatians, who were only schismatics, should be re-baptized when being received into the Church. For Saint Cyprian, the baptism of schismatics upon being received into the Church was not re-baptism at all, but precisely baptism. "We maintain," he wrote to Quintus, "that we do not re-baptize those who come from there, but we baptize; for they have received nothing there where there is nothing."[51] He adds that baptism outside the Church is only "an empty and impure immersion."[52] "There, people are not washed, but are only profaned more; sins are not cleansed but are only redoubled. Such a birth promotes children to the devil and not to God."[53]

Saint Cyprian's conviction about the invalidity of any baptism outside the Church, and about the necessity of once again baptizing all converts to the Church, was confirmed by a local council of the Church which met at Carthage in 256 A.D. with Cyprian himself presiding. In his summation of the council's decisions, the Saint says: "Heretics must be baptized by a baptism solely of the Church so that they can change from enemies to friends and from antichrists to Christians."[54]

The above-stated views of Saint Cyprian which, evidently, the entire Carthagenian Council shared, clearly and profoundly witness how totally fused the Church was with Christianity and vice versa, in the third century.

Not all the views of Saint Cyprian were completely accepted by the Church. In particular, his teaching about the necessity to re-baptize even schismatics upon their conversion to the Church was modified. On this point, the views of Blessed Augustine differ somewhat, although his view of the relationship of Christianity to the Church remains exactly the same.

Blessed Augustine held that the Christian teaching, understood theoretically, can be preserved outside the Church. Truth remains truth even though an evil person might express it. For even the demons confessed Christ just as did the Apostle Peter who said "You are the Christ, the Son of the living God" (Matt 16:16; cf. Matt 8:29).[55] Gold is doubtlessly good and it remains gold even when taken by a thief, even though it serves different aims for him.[56] Christ once said to his disciples, "he who is not against us is on our side" (Luke 9:50). From this it is concluded that one who stands outside the Church on some things is not against the Church and has something of the Church's wealth.[57] Athenians, however, honored the Unknown God: "for as I was passing through and considering the objects of your worship, I even found an altar with this inscription: TO THE UNKNOWN GOD. Therefore, the One whom you worship without knowing, Him I proclaim to you ..." (Acts 17:23). The Apostle James testified that "even the demons believe—and tremble" (James 2:19), and they, of course, are outside of the Church.[58] In his works against the Donatists,[59] Blessed Augustine argues in detail for the validity of schismatic baptism. If, however, it is possible to preserve true teaching outside the Church and if even the sacraments performed in schism from the Church are valid, then is the Church really necessary? Is salvation not possible outside the Church? Does not Blessed Augustine make a distinction between Christianity and the Church? To all these questions a negative reply is given in the system of Blessed Augustine. He ascribes Christian life, which leads to salvation, only to the Church. Outside the Church this life cannot exist.

All the wealth of the Church which is possessed by those who have separated themselves from the Church brings them absolutely no benefit, but only harm.[60] Why is this so? Because, answers Blessed Augustine, all those who have separated from the Church do not possess love. Christ gave a sign by which it is possible to recognize His disciples. This sign is not Christian teaching, not even the sacraments, but only love. Thus, He told His followers, "By this all will know that you are My disciples, if you have love for one another" (John 13:35). The Mysteries will not save if the one receiving them has no love. The Apostle Paul says, "And though I have the gift of prophecy, and understand all mysteries … but have not love, I am nothing" (1 Cor 13:2).[61] Even Caiaphas prophesied, but he was condemned (cf. John 11:49–52).[62] The act of separation from the Church is itself the greatest sin, which proves that schismatics do not have love.[63] One who is reborn in baptism, but does not unite with the Church receives no benefit from baptism because he possesses no love; baptism can be beneficial for him only when he unites with the Church.[64] The Grace of baptism cannot cleanse from sin one who does not belong to the Church; its actions are as if paralyzed by the obstinacy of a schismatic heart in the evil of schism.[65] Since one who is baptized outside the Church displays his sinfulness and the absence of love in him immediately after baptism by entering into the darkness of schism, the sins quickly return upon him. The fact that forgiven sins return if there is no brotherly love is clearly pointed out by the Lord in his Parable of the Unforgiving Servant (cf. Matt 18:21–35) when He spoke of the servant whose master forgave him the debt of ten thousand talents. When this same servant did not take pity upon one of his fellow servants who owed him only one hundred dinars, the master demanded the debtor pay all that was owed to the master. Just as this servant had received forgiveness of the debt for a time, so one who is baptized outside the Church is also freed from his sins for a time. Since, however he remains outside the Church even after baptism, all the sins which he committed before being baptized are again imposed upon him. His sins are forgiven only when he, through love, unites with the Church.[66] Schismatics are deprived of the hope of salvation not only because their baptism is invalid, but also because they are outside the Church and in enmity with it.[67] The Grace of the Holy Spirit can be received and preserved only by one who is united in love with the Church.[68] He who has separated from the Church does not have love. He who does not love the unity of the Church does not have God's love,[69]—it is in vain that he declares that he has the love of Christ.[70] Love can be preserved only in the presence of unity with the Church,[71] because the Holy Spirit revives only the body of the Church.[72] There can be no lawful and sufficient reason to separate from the Church;[73] he who separates from the Church does not possess the Holy Spirit,[74] just as a severed member of the body does not possess the spirit of life, even though it preserves its former identity for some time.[75] Thus, while all those who have separated from the Church oppose it, they cannot be good; although their behavior might appear to be praiseworthy—the very fact of their separation from the Church makes them evil.[76]

Thus, according to the teaching of Blessed Augustine, the Church is a concept narrower than Christianity which is understood only in the sense of abstract theses. It is possible to be in accord with these abstract theses while still remaining outside the Church; but for unity with the Church, the accord of will is indispensable (*consensio voluntatum*). It is evident that without this latter, abstract accord with Christian teaching alone is completely useless and that there is no salvation outside the Church.

The points of view of Saint Cyprian and Blessed Augustine can be seen to differ somewhat, but they both arrive at exactly the same conclusion: outside the Church there is no salvation! People are saved by their love which is the Grace of the New Testament.[77] Outside the Church it is impossible to preserve love,[78] because it is impossible to receive the Holy Spirit.[79]

What have we discovered in these representative examples of Church thought from the third to the fifth century? We have found that they coincide with the conclusions we reached earlier while examining the New Testament teaching about the Church, and the facts of early Christianity. Christianity and the Church are the same thing only when we do not regard Christianity as the sum of a sort of abstract thesis that does not require anything of anyone. Such an understanding of Christianity could only be called demonic. It would follow that such Christians also acknowledge God in the same way as the demons who "believe—and tremble" (Jas 2: 19). Does to know the system really mean to be a true Christian? A servant who knows the will of the master and who does not fulfill it, will be dismissed and rejected and, of course, justly so.

"Christianity is not in the silent conviction, but in the grandeur of the deed," says Saint Ignatius.[80]

Christ is not only a great teacher; He is the Saviour of the world, Who gave mankind new strength, Who renewed mankind. It is not a teaching only that we have received from Christ our Saviour, but life. One is to understand Christianity as a new life, not according to the elements of the world which knows only the principles of egoism and self-love. If one understands Christianity according to Christ with His teaching and model of self-denial and love, then Christianity will necessarily coincide completely with the Church.

To be a Christian means to belong to the Church, for Christianity is precisely the Church. Outside the Church there is no life and there cannot be.

Finally, in order to understand how important the concept of the Church is, it is sufficient to look attentively at the Symbol of Faith (the Creed), for the various articles were introduced into the Symbol of Faith after the appearance of various heretics who distorted one or another truth. Thus the whole Symbol of Faith can be called polemical. Its history reveals that its contents were enlarged as the result of the struggle with one heresy or another.

Such is not the case, however, with the ninth article, which concerns the Church. This article was found in the Symbol of Faith from the very beginning. It was introduced independently of the appearance of any sort of false doctrine. At that time there were still no Protestants who dreamt of some sort of churchless Christianity.

It is clear that, from the very beginning, the concept of the Church lay at the head of Christian beliefs and that this truth, that Christianity is specifically the Church, can be considered to have been given from the Lord Jesus Christ Himself.

Having risen to this height of Church consciousness, it will be of great benefit to look at contemporary life, at the trends and opinions which are widespread in it and to give them an appraisal from the point of view of the Church.

POINTS OF REFLECTION

1. How does Christ's prayer for the unity of believers found in John 17 inform our understanding of the Church?

2. In what way does the Apostle Paul use the "body" as an image of the Church?

3. How does secular society deal with individual egoism in order to achieve good civic order? What distinguishes a united Christian community from a unified secular group?

4. What does the Kingdom of God provide that a temporal society cannot?

5. What harm can occur when Christians uncon-
   sciously assimilate opinions about the Faith and
   Truth that come from outside the teaching of the
   Church?

6. How does the third person of the Trinity—the
   Holy Spirit—work in the Christian community
   to bring unity?

7. How do St Cyprian of Carthage and Blessed
   Augustine differ in their understanding of
   non-Orthodox baptisms?

PART II

The Place of the Church

The Nicene Creed

(1) I believe in one God, the Father Almighty, Maker of heaven and earth and all things visible and invisible;

(2) and in one Lord Jesus Christ, the Son of God, the Only-begotten, begotten of the Father before all ages;

(3) Light of Light, true God of true God, begotten, not made, of one essence with the Father, by Whom all things were made;

(4) Who for us men and for our salvation came down from the Heavens, and was incarnate of the Holy Spirit and the Virgin Mary, and became man; and was crucified for us under Pontius Pilate, and suffered, and was buried;

(5) and arose on the third day according to the Scriptures;

(6)   and ascended into the heavens, and sitteth at the right hand of the Father;

(7)   and shall come again, with glory, to judge both the living and the dead, Whose kingdom shall have no end.

(8)   And in the Holy Spirit, the Lord, the Giver of Life, Who proceedeth from the Father, Who with the Father and the Son together is worshipped and glorified, Who spake by the prophets.

(9)   In one Holy, Catholic, and Apostolic Church.

(10) I confess one baptism for the remission of sins.

(11) I look for the resurrection of the dead;

(12) and the life of the age to come.

Amen.[81]

"I believe in One, Holy, Catholic and Apostolic Church" (The ninth article of the Nicene Creed). Thus every Orthodox Christian confesses his faith in the great truth of the Church. But it is hardly possible to point out any other article of the Symbol of Faith which is less understood by the heart of man who has read it with his lips than is the ninth article wherein the truth of the Church is expressed. This is, in part, understandable: for in the ninth article of the Symbol of Faith, man confesses his bond with the visible community of the followers of Christ. By this, in these short words of confession, he agrees with all the truths taught by the Church as she is acknowledged as the custodian of Christ's teaching. From the practical side, the agreement is given, once and for all, to be submissive to all those laws by which the Church reaches the aims of its existence, and according to which it is governed as a society living on earth. Thus it seems that man will not err if he express the thought that the truth of the Church, above all other truths, touches the very life of each Christian, defining not only his beliefs, but also his life. To acknowledge the Church means more than just dreaming about Christ. It means living in a Christian manner and following the path of love and self-denial. The truth of the Church, therefore, is contrary to those principles of life that have slowly crept into the consciousness and attitude even of the Russian religious community, though for the most part, among the so-called intellectual society. During the reign of Peter the Great, known as *the sorrowful times* for the Church, the upper strata of Russian society drew away from the life of the Church people and began to live a life in common with all the other European peoples rather than with the Russians. While submitting to Western influence in all spheres of life, Russian society could not avoid the influence of Western confessions upon the formation of its religious attitudes. These confessions were referred to, with good reason, as "heresies against the dogma and essence of the Church and against its faith in itself," by a true son of the Orthodox Church and fatherland, Alexei Stepanovich Khomiakov. It was not in error that he considered the denial of the Church the most characteristic feature of both Roman Catholicism and Protestantism.

The truth of the Church was greatly distorted in the West after Rome had fallen away from the Church. In the West, God's kingdom began to be viewed more as an earthly kingdom. Latinism obscured the Christian concept of the Church in the consciousness of its members with its legalistic account of good deeds, its mercenary relationship to God and its falsification of salvation.

Latinism gave birth to a legitimate, although very insubordinate, offspring in the form of Protestantism. Protestantism was created from the soil of humanism which was not a religious phenomenon; on the contrary, all its leading ideas are purely earthly—human. It created respect for man in his natural condition. Protestantism, having carried over the basis of humanism into the religious field, was not the protest of a genuine ancient Church Christian consciousness against those forms and norms which were created by medieval Papism, as Protestant theologians are often inclined to claim. Far from it; Protestantism was a protest on the very same plane. It did not re-establish ancient Christianity, it only replaced one distortion of Christianity with another, and the new falsehood was much worse than the first. Protestantism became the last word in Papism, and brought it to its logical conclusion. Truth and salvation are bestowed upon love that is the Church—such is Church consciousness. Latinism, having fallen away from the Church, changed this consciousness and proclaimed: truth is given to the separate person of the Pope, and the Pope manages the salvation of all. Protestantism only objected: Why is truth given to the Pope alone?—and added: truth and salvation—independent of the Church—are open to each separate individual. Every individual was thus promoted to the rank of an infallible Pope. Protestantism placed a papal tiara on every German professor and, with its countless number of popes, completely destroyed the concept of the Church by substituting faith with the reason of each separate personality. It substituted salvation in the Church with a dreamy confidence in salvation through Christ in egoistic isolation from the Church.

From the very beginning, in practice, Protestants departed from and by roundabout ways (contraband so to speak) introduced some elements of the dogma about the Church, having recognized some authorities, although only in the area of dogma. Being a religious anarchy, pure Protestantism, like all anarchies, turned out to be completely impossible, and by that, testified before us to the indisputable truth that the human soul is Church-prone by nature.

Still, the theoretical side of Protestantism appealed to human self-love and self-will of all varieties, for self-love and self-will received a sort of sanctification and blessing from Protestantism. This fact is revealed today in the endless dividing and factionalism of Protestantism itself. It is Protestantism that openly proclaimed the greatest lie of all: that one can be a Christian while denying the Church. Nevertheless, by tying its members by some obligatory authorities and church laws, Protestantism entangles itself in a hopeless contradiction: having itself separated the individual from the Church, it nevertheless places limits on that freedom. From this stems the constant mutiny of Protestants against those few and pitiful remnants of Church consciousness which are still preserved by the official representatives of their denominations.

It is easy to understand that Protestantism corresponds to the almost completely pagan outlook generally approved of in the West. There, where the cult of individualism blossoms luxuriantly, finding prophets in fashionable philosophy and sophisticated literature that is an end in itself, Christ's ideal of the Church can, of course, have no place; for His ideal negates self-love and self-will in people and demands love from them all.

There is a direct influence of Protestantism in our contemporary Russian society. All of our Russian rationalistic sectarianism has its ideological roots in Protestantism, from which it descends directly. After all, where do all the sectarian missionaries come from if not from the Protestant countries? All the points of discord between these sectarians and the Orthodox Church come from the denial of the Church in the name of an imaginary "Evangelical Christianity."

However, many now come, independently of Protestantism, to a denial of the Church, assimilating, in general, a western European attitude which developed outside the Church and that is completely alien and even hostile to the spirit of the Church.

More and more of that haughty western European ideology of self-love penetrates into our community. Russian literature which formerly taught love and moral rebirth, especially in the works of the great Dostoevsky, has, in recent years, in the persons of, for example, Gorky, Andreyev, and others like them, begun to bow to a western European Baal, the god of proud individualism.

When, in our Orthodox society, love is forced out by pride and self-love (which is called "noble"—although the holy Fathers of the Church speak of self-love and pride only in connection with the devil), when self-denial is substituted by self-assertion, and meek obedience is replaced by proud self-will, then a dense fog, inseparably linked with directly opposite ideals, shrouds the truth of the Church.

During the course of many years, Russian people have gotten out of the habit of being Church-minded and have begun to lose the knowledge of the Church as a new life in Christ. There was a better time when Ivan Tikhonovich Pososhkov bequeathed to his son this charge: "I, my son, strongly bequeath and adjure you, with all your strength, to adhere to the Holy Eastern Church as the mother who has given you birth… and tear yourself from all who are enemies of the Holy Church and do not have any friendly relations with them since they are the enemies of God."[82] According to the mind of Pososhkov, an enemy of the Church is, without fail, an enemy of God. Many people have already lost such clearness of thought and, little by little, the most terrible forgery of Christ's faith has been formed in our days. They have looked upon the faith from a purely abstract point of view as a collection of teachings upon which it is possible to carry out various experiments. Christianity, in the sense of Church life and of mankind re-born through Christ the Saviour, is almost forgotten.

Christ Himself said "I will build My church" (Matt 16:18); but does one now speak of this Church? No; now they prefer to speak of Christianity; moreover they consider Christianity to be some kind of philosophical or moral teaching. Christianity—it sounds like neo-Kantianism or Nietzchianism! This substitution of the Church with Christianity, like a subtle venom, penetrates into the consciousness of even the Church community. It is a subtle poison because it is hidden under a flowery covering of loud speeches about the defects of "historical Christianity" (i.e., the Church), about how it does not seem to correspond with some sort of "pure," "evangelical" Christianity. The Gospel and Christ are contrasted with the Church, which, for some reason, is called "historical" as if there is or ever was a different "non-historical" Church. The truth is, however, that Satan has taken on the image of an angel of light. He makes it appear as though he is concerned about the well-being of Christ's truth, as if he wants to cleanse Christ's truth from the untruth of mankind. One automatically recalls the wise dictum of the venerable Vincent of Lerins: "When we hear some persons cite the apostolic or prophetic sayings in refutation of the Catholic faith, we must not doubt that the devil is speaking through their lips; and in order to creep undetected among the open-hearted sheep they hide their wolves' appearance while retaining their wolves' ferocity. They clothe themselves with sayings from the divine Scriptures, like the fleece of sheep, so that, feeling the softness of the wool, no one will fear their sharp teeth."[83]

> Christianity, in the sense of Church life and of mankind re-born through Christ the Saviour, is almost forgotten.

In actual fact, these attempts to set the Gospel into opposition with the Church and substitute the Church with an uncertain concept of Christianity have produced many lamentable results: Christian life is drying up. It appears as only one more teaching in the endless series of ancient and new teachings; and a very indefinite teaching at that, for without the Church the possibility is open for an innumerable quantity of the most arbitrary and mutually contradictory understandings. In this respect, Christianity stands incomparably lower than many philosophical schools. In actual fact, the founders of philosophical schools have left whole volumes of their compositions behind. They have left more or less clear expositions of their systems, they have more or less fully expressed themselves so that there is no limitless space for various arbitrary interpretations of their teaching. The Lord Jesus Christ did not leave His system. He wrote nothing. Only once is it said of Him that He wrote with His finger, and even that time He wrote only on the ground (cf. John 8:6).

Thus there is nothing easier than to reinterpret Christ's teaching according to one's personal taste and to invent "Christianity," passing off, under this name, the dreams of one's heart and the images of one's own idle fantasy.

The sacred books of the New Testament were written by practical, unscholarly apostles. Throughout the centuries there have been "correctors of the Apostles," as Saint Irenaeus of Lyons calls them,[84] ones who considered themselves higher than the Apostles who were Galilean fishermen. Does it become a highly educated European of the twentieth century to accept on faith all that is said by some "fishermen"? So many free themselves from the authority of the Apostles and desire to interpret Christ's teaching while being guided only by their personal whims. For example, Leo Tolstoy bluntly declared that the Apostle Paul did not properly understand Christ's teaching;[85] it follows that Tolstoy considered himself to be higher than the Apostle Paul. One can marvel greatly at how far people go in their "interpretation" of Christianity. Whatever they might desire, they immediately find in the Gospel. It would appear that it is possible to cover one's every idle dream and even ill-intentioned thought by means of the Gospel's authority.

No, the faith of Christ becomes clear and definite for man only when he unhypocritically believes in the Church; only then are the pearls of this faith clear; only then does the faith remain free from the pile of dirty

rubbish of all the possible, self-willed opinions and judgments. The Apostle Paul had already spoken of this when
he called the Church of the living God "the pillar and
ground of the truth" (1 Tim 3:15).

Christian teaching separated from the Church appears
to be something very indefinite, illusive, and constantly
changing according to desire.

To misrepresent the relationship of the Church with
Christianity leads to another misinterpretation—the dis-
torting of Christ the God-man to merely the man Jesus
of Nazareth. Just as the faith in the Church is inseparably
linked with the acknowledgment of the divinity of Christ
the Saviour, so the denial of the Church unfailingly leads
ultimately to the denial of the incarnation of the Son of
God, the denial of the divinity of Jesus Christ. It is not at
all necessary for Him to be a God-man in order to give
some kind of teaching. Christ's state of being God-man
is necessary only when He is seen as the Saviour, Who
poured out strength into human nature and Who founded
the Church. In actual fact, this inseparable tie between the
truth of the Church and the truth of His being the Son
of God is seen from the words of Jesus Christ Himself.
Simon Peter said: "You are the Christ, the Son of the living God." Then Jesus responded saying to him "You are
Peter, and on this rock [that is on the truth of the incarnation of God which Peter confessed] I will build My
church; and the gates of Hades shall not prevail against

it" (Matt 16:16,18). The ancient Church, in a special effort, with all its strength, defined this truth of the incarnate Son of God as one in essence with God the Father, because it thirsted for a real renewal of human nature, for the re-creation of the "new creature," that is of the Church. The internal motivating force of all the dogmatic movements of the fourth century was the unshakable belief in the fact that the Son of God is the second person of the Holy Trinity, Who came down to earth, became man, revealed the mysteries of the Kingdom of God, founded His Church on earth, suffered for the sins of mankind, and, having conquered death, arose from the dead, opening the path for the deification of man, not only in soul, but in body.[86] Why was the battle with Arianism so strenuous? Why were the Arians met with such rejection that Saint Athanasius the Great, a pillar of Christ's Church, refused them the name of "Christian"? To the irreligious contemporary man, all the dogmatic arguments of the fourth century seem incomprehensible and senseless. This was, nevertheless, a struggle between two extremely contradictory views of Christ—the mystical-religious view in which He is the source of life, salvation, immortality, and the deification of man, as opposed to the rationalistic view in which Christ is represented only as an idolized teacher and a model example for his followers. The center of the issue was: In the future, will Christianity remain a religion with all the totality of its pure beliefs and hopes, or will it be reduced to a simple philosophy with religious nuances, of which there were many at that time? These questions concerning the divinity of the Son of God, which affected the most intimate side of the believing soul, were discussed in the squares and the marketplaces.[87] One can say that even then the Church defended the truth that its Founder is one in essence with God the Father. The Arians, people of a rationalistic mentality, denied the one-essence of the incarnated Son of God, looking upon Him as the founder of some school, who, therefore, does not necessarily have to be perfect God. The desire to be a "new creature," a "renewed nature," that is to say, a Church of the living God, demands the recognition of the full divinity of Christ. "God became man so that man may become god."[88] "The Son of God became the Son of man, that man, having been taken into the Word, and receiving the adoption, might become the son of God."[89] Thus did Saint Athanasius the Great and Saint Irenaeus of Lyons define the concept of the incarnation of God.[90] The theology of our Orthodox Church is filled with such definitions. Here are examples from the service of the Nativity of Christ:

"Today God has come to earth, and man ascends to heaven. . . . Man was created in God's image and likeness, but when Jesus saw him fallen through transgression, He bowed the heavens and came down, dwelling in a virgin womb, without forsaking His divinity. Adam, once corrupted, was refashioned. He cried out 'Glory to Thine appearing, my Redeemer and my God.'" (Litia, Stichera)[91];

"Sing and dance for joy, for Christ has come to restore us and to save our souls" (The stichera of "Glory" at the Aposticha)[92];

"Man was made in the image of God, but he sinned, and lost immortality. He fell from the divine and better life, enslaved completely by corruption. Now the wise Creator fashions him again, for He has been glorified!" (The Canon, Ode I).[93]

The Orthodox Church is the bearer of the concept of the actual, true salvation of man, of his full re-birth, renewal, re-creation, and deification, which man cannot attain by his own strength no matter how much he might philosophize.

The incarnation of the Son of God is absolutely essential for the Church in order for it to be the Church—a society of renewed humanity. Thus for the people of the Church, who have perceived the whole height of the religious ideal of the holy Church, Jesus Christ always was and is the Son of God, of one essence with God the Father.

"Others," writes St Irenaeus, "reject the coming of the Son of God and the dispensation of His incarnation, which the apostles delivered and the prophets declared beforehand, even such as should be the summing up of mankind … such also are reckoned amongst those who are lacking in faith."[94]

At the time of Saint Irenaeus, some false teachers were asserting that the entire matter of Christ consisted only in that He gave a new law in place of the ancient, which He abolished. Saint Irenaeus, on the other hand, asserted that neither the new law nor the new teaching was the aim of Christ's advent, but its aim was the re-creation of the fallen human nature. "If," he writes, "there arises within you such a thought: 'What new thing did the Lord bring with His advent?' then know that He brought everything new. He brought Himself and thus renewed and gave life to mankind."[95]

If anyone denies the Church with its religious ideals, then Christ becomes for him only a teacher-philosopher in the category of Buddha, Confucius, Socrates, Lao-Tse, and others. Moreover, Christ, as a teacher, appears to be far from original. Complaisant scholarship cites a multitude of various sources, including Babylonian myths, from which Christ's teachings are supposedly borrowed. Christ is likened to a poor scholar who compiles his work by borrowing, not always successfully, from the works of various other people.

The enemies of Christianity gloatingly point to the results of scientific research and declare that, in essence, Jesus of Nazareth did not even give a new teaching; He only repeated what had been said even without Him.

For those who believe in Christ, however, all this talk about various "influences" on Christianity is completely senseless. The essence of Christ's activities, as we have seen, is not at all in teaching, but in salvation. "God has sent His only begotten Son into the world, that we might live through Him" (1 John 4:9). "I have written to you who believe in the name of the Son of God, that you may know that you have eternal life" (1 John 5:13).

Even though insights of truth which are close to Christianity can be found in the teachings of earthly philosophers, it was Christ Who renewed human nature, created the Church, sent down the Holy Spirit and thus established the beginning of a new life which no mortal philosopher could do. The descent to earth of the Son of God and His death on the cross were indispensable for the creation of the Church; and all those who separate Christianity from the Church sooner or later blaspheme by denying Christ the God-man because the divinity of Christ becomes unnecessary for them.

It was Christ Who renewed human nature, created the Church, sent down the Holy Spirit and thus established the beginning of a new life.

There are an increasing number of people among us who dream of some sort of churchless Christianity. These people have a seemingly constant anarchical system of thought. They are either incapable, or, more often, simply too lazy to think through to the end of their thoughts.

Without even speaking of the most evident contradictions of the churchless quasi-Christianity, it is always possible to see that it is completely void of the genuine Grace of Christian life, and the inspiration and quickening of the Spirit.

When people forget that the Church gave them the Gospel book, then the Scriptures become like the Koran which is said to have been dropped from the sky by Allah. When they somehow contrive to overlook the teaching about the Church in the Bible, then all that remains of Christianity is a teaching that is powerless to re-create life and man, as is every philosophical system.

Our forebears, Adam and Eve, sought to become "like gods" without God, relying on the magical power of the beautiful "apple." This is how many of our contemporaries dream of being saved: with the Gospel, but without the Church and without the God-man. They hope on the book of the Gospel exactly as Adam and Eve hoped on the apple in paradise. The book, however, does not have the power to give them a new life. People who deny the Church constantly speak about "evangelical principles," about evangelical teaching; but Christianity as life is completely alien to them.

In the churchless form, Christianity is only a sound, now and then sentimental, but is always a caricature and lifeless. It is precisely these people who, denying the Church, have made Christianity, in the words of V. S. Soloviev, "deathly boring." As David Strauss observed, "When the edifice of the Church is destroyed and, on the bare, poorly leveled place, there is erected only the edifying sermon, the result is sad and terrible."[96]

In the past, our most consistent preacher of churchless Christianity was Leo Tolstoy. Tolstoy confused many with his preaching, but it is in the example of Tolstoyism that one can clearly observe the insolvency of Christianity without the Church. The initial point in the false teaching of Tolstoy can be called his sharp separation of Christianity from the Church. Tolstoy had roundly condemned the Church, while at the same time admiring Christianity. For him, however, Christianity immediately became only a teaching, and Christ, only a teacher. When any kind of teaching is placed before us, it is not that important for us to know whose teaching it is. For Tolstoy, the living person of Christ lost all significance and meaning. Having taken Christ's teaching, it appeared possible to forget about Christ Himself.

Tolstoy denied the God-man, referring to Him as "a crucified Jew,"—"a dead Jew." With that, the Gospel is severed from its very beginning where the proclamation is made of the supernatural birth of the Son of God from the Virgin Mary, and it is severed from its end where the resurrection of the Son of God from the dead and His ascension into heaven is recorded. Tolstoy did not limit himself to this cutting off of the Gospel from its beginning and its end; he also restructured its "middle" according to his own tastes. He thus compelled his Jesus to say only what he, the teacher of Yasnaya Polyana (the name of Leo Tolstoy's estate), commanded.

Christ Himself promised to send His disciples "another Comforter." "It is to your advantage that I go away; for if I do not go away, the [Comforter] will not come to you; but if I depart, I will send Him to you" (John 16:7). "The [Comforter], the Holy Spirit, whom the Father will send in My name, He will teach you all things, and bring to your remembrance all things that I said to you" (John 14:26). This "Comforter," the Divine Advocate, is honored by the Church of Christ as the source of the new, abundant Church life which is the gift of Grace. The Apostle Paul, as we have seen, constantly speaks of the Holy Spirit living in the Church.

Nevertheless, Tolstoy denied the Holy Spirit. He called the Orthodox Church not Christ's but, mockingly, "the Holy Spirit's." He then stooped to blaspheming the Holy Mysteries through which a member of the Church receives the grace of the Holy Spirit for a new life. Baptism is a mystery of rebirth—for Tolstoy it became "the bathing of infants." The Holy Eucharist, without which, according to the teaching of Christ Himself, one cannot have life within oneself (cf. John 6:53), became, in the blasphemous terminology of Tolstoy, "soup" which one "swallows from a little spoon." One can thank Tolstoy for at least being consistent. Having limited all of Christ's work to His teaching alone and, having denied the Church, it was a logical necessity for Tolstoy to come to that all of his conclusions destroyed Christianity itself. At least Tolstoy clearly demonstrated for us what result to expect from the absurd separation of Christianity from the Church and the negation of the Church in the name of imaginary Christianity. If one is to separate Christianity from the Church, then there is no need for the divinity of the Saviour and the Holy Spirit is unnecessary.

Without the Holy Spirit, however, and without the divinity of the Saviour, without the incarnation of the Son of God, the teaching of Jesus the Nazarene becomes of little value for life, just as any other teaching; for it is impossible to share the Socratic optimism, according to which knowledge is virtue.

The insolvency of Tolstoy's churchless understanding of Christianity is evident from the fact that Tolstoyism created no kind of life. Christianity is possible only in union with the living God-man Christ, and in the Grace-created union of people with the Church. In Tolstoyism there is neither one nor the other.

> Christianity is possible only in union with the living God-man Christ, and in the Grace-created union of people with the Church.

Instead of the enthusiasm of the martyrs and ascetics of the Church, instead of the bond of love which binds the Apostles and believers so strongly that they have "one heart and one soul," the followers of Tolstoy produced only grotesque and lifeless "Tolstoyite colonies."

"He who has the Son has life; he who does not have the Son of God does not have life" (1 John 5:12). As V. S. Soloviev said, Tolstoy united around himself only a few dozen stupid people of the sort who are always ready to scatter in various directions. "The Great Teacher" Tolstoy, it appears, taught nothing to anyone and the tale of the "green stick" saved no one because it is not a stick but the cross of Christ which is necessary for salvation.[97] Thus, using Tolstoyism as an example, we see that churchless Christianity leads to a terrible distortion and even to the destruction of Christianity itself. It is refuted by its own complete lifelessness.

Protestant false teaching is disgraced by this same lifelessness. What have the Protestants attained, having obscured the concept of the Church with their philos-ophizing? They have attained only disunity, and most hopeless disunity. Protestantism is constantly breaking down into more sects. There is no Protestant Church life, but some sort of "scarcely living" life of separate sects and communities. Protestantism has killed the general Church life, about which the Lord Jesus Christ prayed in that first sacred prayer.

In actual fact, the fundamentalist Protestants stand far closer to Orthodox Christians than do the Protestants of extreme rationalistic doctrines who have nothing in common with Christianity, except for the arbitrary and baseless assuming of the name. They do not even seek a blessing for that. What kind of unity is possible between them? What kind of life can they have?

We are not saying all this entirely from ourselves. In some moments of enlightenment, Protestants themselves say the very same thing even more sharply. "The country," writes one of them, "which was the cradle of the Refor-mation is becoming the grave of the Reformationist faith. The Protestant faith is on the verge of death. All the latest works about Germany, just as all personal observations, agree in this."[98] "Is it not noticeable in our contemporary theology that its representatives have lost everything pos-itive?" another of them asks.[99] Still sadder are the words of a third. "The vital strength of Protestantism is being exhausted in a muddle of dogmatic schools, theological discord, church strife. . . . the Reformation is forgotten or is held in contempt; God's word, for which fathers died, is being subjected to doubts; Protestantism is disunited, weak and powerless."[100]

An Orthodox researcher of Lutheranism ends his work with this dismal conclusion. "Left to their own devices, their own subjective reason and faith, Lutherans courageously went ahead on a false path, and autodidactically perverted Christianity, perverted the symbolic dogma itself, having placed the Lutheran denomination on the edge of ruin. In Lutheranism, the authority of the first reformers is increasingly denied. More and more the community of the faith is being destroyed and Lutheranism is coming closer to its spiritual death."[101]

At the present time, Protestants already openly acknowledge that in Germany not more than a third of the pastors recognize the divinity of Christ. What is this if not a spiritual death, for according to the Apostle John, "He who has the Son has life; he who does not have the Son of God does not have life" (1 John 5:12).

At one time in Moscow there was a great clamor about the "International Christian Student Union." In the very center of Russian Orthodox holy places, there arrived a large number of various missionaries of this union, such as John Raleigh Mott and Miss Raus who addressed the Russian students with English preaching. We also heard a lecture about this overseas union. It was said that the union was non-confessional; in it, freedom was given to every Christian denomination. Denominations unite in the union, according to the terminology of the lecturer, "on a federative basis." Subsequently a form of Christianity independent of the Church is theorized.

This is precisely the reason that the union is something which was born dead. Is there, or can there be any Christian life in such a "union"? If there is, then it is most pitiful. Imagine a "congress" of Christian student organizations at which there appeared "delegates of federative-united denominational fractions," a congress with all its "resolutions," "desires" and so on. If such a union does take place, then how endlessly lower it will be than the genuine Church life of Orthodoxy. Only for a person roaming in some foreign place far from holy Orthodoxy and from all faith can such a barely living life in union on some sort of "federative basis" seem to be a new revelation, a joy for the empty soul! What kind of blessings are these mere flickers of life in comparison with the fullness of the Orthodox universal life!

While I was listening to the lecture on "The International Christian Student Union," my heart was filled with sadness and sorrow. How many sincere people who are thirsty for God, thirsty for life, are perishing of hunger and being fed the suckle of some overseas student union. Can it be that they do not know how to make use of the abundant bread in the home of the heavenly Father, in the Orthodox Church? It is necessary only to forget all the "federative bases," to freely give oneself up to complete obedience to the Orthodox Church and to adhere to the completeness of Church life, to the life of the body of Christ [in order to make use of the abundant bread of the Orthodox Church].

The concept of the Church was wonderfully understood by A. S. Khomiakov, who said that for the Church of Christ unia is impossible, only unity is possible.[102] There have been occasions when frivolous people thought to create an international religion by way of the study-room. Millions of appeals were sent out with the invitation to unite in this "common religion," the project which was credited to these appeals. This scheme, however, was outlined in the most general terminology, under which a Catholic, Protestant, Muslim, or Jew could sign with identical comfort. Of course, if all people would agree to this scheme, it would in no way unite them among each other: general abstract theses would not obligate anyone to anything. People would remain the same; no one would receive salvation. It is complete madness to attempt to unite people on the basis of some teaching. For this a special supernatural power is required, which is possessed only by the One, Holy, Catholic Church of Christ.

It is not at all difficult to answer the question: what do these and other similar phenomena of our contemporary life mean, and on what grounds could they have appeared? The ground for them is the fact that for many of our contemporaries, the genuine Orthodox Christian ideal of the Church appeared to be too lofty. People have now become so stagnated and stiffened in their self-love, that the Orthodox concept of the Church seems to them to be some sort of coercion of personality, an incomprehensible and unnecessary despotism. The Orthodox concept of the Church demands from everyone much self-denial, humility, and love. Thus, in the hearts of our contemporaries, which are impoverished of love and for whom the dearest thing is self-love, this ideal is a burden too uncomfortable to carry.

What is to be done? Oh, mankind knows well how to act in such cases. When an ideal seems to be beyond its strength, too heavy, it is substituted by something more suitable. The true ideal is depreciated and its essence is distorted, although, sometimes, the former name is retained. How many have already given up as hopeless this ideal of love? They say that to build a community life on the basis of this love is a vain dream from which it is better to withdraw early in order to escape failure later.

As if this were not enough, they even condemn as unhealthy and harmful any enthusiasm with the ideal of Church or religious life in general, which would somehow hinder the necessary progress of societal life. Not very long ago when the journal *Vekhi*[103] appeared, the most progressive camp of "public-spirited persons" raised a desperate cry: "Reaction! Reaction!" Having set love aside as useless in public life, something reserved only for the personal needs of man, they turned their attention exclusively to law, with which they thought to cure all human ailments.

Moreover, virtue in general is substituted with order and external propriety and decency. Gold is expensive and so for its substitution they have invented a gilding just as they have thought up propriety and external decency as a substitute for the missing virtue. They conduct themselves in exactly this same way with the ideal of the Church, which demands the complete unity of souls and hearts. They substitute the Church with a Christianity having an indefinite value. Their conscience is not troubled by such an act; "Christianity" is, for all that, still a decent sort of a name.

Without the Church, it is possible to place whatever pleases oneself under this name. In this way you will not completely break with Christ and you will not especially inconvenience yourself. In a word: the wolves are fed, but the sheep are not eaten!

The great misfortune of our time lies in the fact that no one wishes to admit frankly to their own spiritual poverty and that their hearts have been hardened to such a degree that Christ's ideal of the Church has become burdensome and even unintelligible. No, having copper instead of gold, they now wish to declare gold valueless. Now they assault the Church with bitterness and deny the very concept of the Church, hypocritically taking refuge in loud and stereotypically beautiful, tedious phrases about "personal freedom" and "individual interpretation" of Christianity and about a religion of freedom and spirit.

Christ's ideal of a single Church community ("I do not pray for these alone, but also for those who will believe in Me through their word; that they all may be one, as You, Father, are in Me, and I in You; that they also may be one in Us, that the world may believe that You sent Me" [John 17:20–21]) appears to them to be a distortion and a disfigurement and thus it loses its vital meaning.

Churchless Christianity, the so-called evangelical Christianity, and assorted world Christian student unions—all this is nothing other than a debasement and distortion of Christ's concept of the Church, killing all genuine Christian, Grace-filled Church life.

Are these things which we have spoken about, however, the only phenomena that testify to the insufficiency in the contemporary understanding of the unbreakable bond of Christianity with the Church? We meet with this lack of comprehension at absolutely every step. Now people who think about God in general, people who are hardly interested in religious questions, who try to establish themselves in life without any living faith, nevertheless consider it a duty of propriety, as it were, to speak out in respect to Christianity. Their words, of course, resound with manifest falseness and hypocrisy.

We have not yet encountered a full and open contempt for Christianity—this limit has been reached by only a few who are oppressed by the devil (cf. Acts 10:37–38), the "progressives" (if, of course, one considers the direction of hell progress).

The ordinary "man-in-the-street" usually speaks about Christianity with a certain amount of respect. "Christianity, oh! that, of course, is a lofty and great teaching. Who is arguing against that?" This rough approval is how one speaks of Christianity while, at the same time, it is seemingly considered a sign of good form to be in some sort of often unconscious opposition to everything of the Church.

In the souls of many, a respect for Christianity somehow manages to coexist with a disdain for the Church. Such people are not embarrassed to call themselves Christians at least, but they do not want to hear about the Church and are ashamed to display any Church consciousness in any way. People who, according to their birth certificates, are "of the Orthodox Faith," with a strange malicious delight, point to the actual and, more often, imaginary shortcomings in Church life. They do not grieve about these shortcomings, in accordance with the commandment of the Apostle Paul, "if one member suffers, all the members suffer with it" (1 Cor 12:26), on the contrary, they gloat.

In the so-called progressive press, there are many persons who earn their living almost exclusively from slander against the Church institutions and representatives of the Church hierarchy. Slander against everything of the Church has now become, for some, merely a profitable trade. Nevertheless, many hurry to believe these notorious falsehoods without any hesitation. Unkind people, having heard something evil about their enemies, rush to believe all of its evilness, fearing lest its evil be proven untrue.

This is precisely what one must constantly observe among people in their relationship to the Church. Thus, again we see how widely spread is the notion of the separation of Christianity from the Church: they consider themselves to be Christians but they want to hear nothing of the Church.

In surroundings far removed from the faith in general, there is an inconceivable confusion of notions. When people who are far from the Church begin to judge it, it can be clearly seen that they have absolutely no understanding of the essence of Christianity and the Church and thus the very virtues of the Church appear to them as its deficiencies. As an example, how many outbursts of blind enmity towards the Church did the death of Tolstoy (that is the refusal of the Church to bury him) provoke? But is the Church guilty of the fact that Tolstoy departed from it, having become its obvious and dangerous enemy? He, you see, tore himself from the Church, as a visible society, even considering it to be a harmful institution.

If the Church kept such members, however, would this not mean for the Church to deny itself? What, therefore, is the meaning of all these attacks against the Church in the press, at meetings, and in conversations? Reason absolutely refuses to understand all this. It is completely impossible to find even the most remote rationality in the speeches and actions which one had occasion to listen to and read about. Every political party retains the right to excommunicate from itself members who have betrayed the party views and who have begun to act in a manner harmful to the party. Only the Orthodox Church, for some reason, cannot excommunicate one who himself has departed from it and has become its enemy. Yet, who would begin to reproach and abuse any of the social-democrats or cadets because they had stopped interacting with and had publicly denounced a former member after he had gone over to the camp of the monarchists? Yes, we have observed the blind and senseless outbursts of satanic malice against the Holy Church; but saddest of all is the fact that many have abused the Church in the name of Christianity. Thousands of times one has read: "Here they have excommunicated Tolstoy, but was he not a true Christian?" Forgetting all the blasphemy of Tolstoy and his denial of Christ the God-man, such speeches are repeated not only by professional newspaper liars but also by people who were evidently sincere.

Again we are presented with the idea, firmly embedded in contemporary minds, of the possibility of some sort of "true Christianity" without the Church or even sharply hostile to it. Could anything like this be possible if the idea of the Church was clear, if it had not been substituted by some other completely unintelligible and indefinite values?

Can anyone imagine that in the apostolic period, the Christian Church would have been subjected to any kind of reproaches on the part of heathens because it excommunicated unfit members, heretics for example, from itself? In the first centuries, nevertheless, excommunication from the Church was the most common measure of Church discipline and everyone considered it to be fully lawful and very useful.

Why was this so? Because then the Church was seen as a clear and definite value, precisely as a Church and not some sort of "Christianity." At that time there was no room for the absurd thought that Christianity is one thing and the Church another, as if Christianity were possible apart from the Church. In those times it was realized that enmity against the Church was also enmity against Christianity. Animosity toward the Church in the name of some sort of supposed Christianity is solely a product of our sorrowful times.

When Christianity appeared before the eyes of the world precisely as a Church, then this "world" itself clearly understood and involuntarily acknowledged that the Church and Christianity are one and the same. Now there is not such a sharp definition sufficient to distinguish the unity of the Church from everyone outside of the Church. Now those in the Church and those who themselves ask to be excommunicated are held on an equal plane. One can truly say that there is no Church discipline: everything has become non-obligatory for the intellectual laity—attendance at divine services, confession, and Holy Communion. Thus the Church has no clear and definite borders which would separate it from "those outside."

Sometimes it seems as if our whole Church is in dispersion, in disorder. One cannot tell who is ours and who is the enemy. Some sort of anarchy is ruling in the minds of many. Too many "teachers" have appeared and a "schism in the body" (1 Cor 12:25) of the Church has occurred. Ancient Church bishops taught from the "high place." Now, one who says of himself that he is only "at the porch" or even only "near the church walls," nevertheless considers himself entitled to teach to the entire Church, including the hierarchy. These people gather and compose all their opinions about Church questions from various "public sheets" (as Metropolitan Philaret used to call newspapers), where items on Church matters are written by defrocked priests and Church renegades of all sorts, or embittered and insolent scoffers (as foretold in 2 Pet 3:3), or people who have no connection with the Church and who feel nothing toward it but animosity.

In such a mass of confusion, many are already asking with concern: "Where is the Church?" That is why in our time there are many varied and fantastic "searchings." In the apostolic age, those who sought the salvation of their souls headed for the Church, and the outsiders did not dare trouble them (cf. Acts 5:13). Then there was no possibility of a question, "where is the Church?" It was a clear and definite value, sharply separated from everything not of the Church. Now there stands some sort of intermediate stage between the Church and the "world" and there is no longer that clear separation: the Church and that which is outside the Church.

There is also some sort of indefinite Christianity and even something else which is not Christianity, but a general abstract religion. These vague concepts of Christianity and religion have darkened the light of the Church so that it is poorly seen by those who seek, which is why "searching" so often now goes over into "wandering."

For this reason there is, in our days, such an abundance of those who are "always learning, and never able to come to the knowledge of the truth" (2 Tim 3:7). A new sport has been created, if we may call it that, a sport of "god-seeking." "God-seeking" has become the goal in itself and if their efforts were ever crowned with success, they would feel themselves highly unfortunate and immediately turn, with their former zeal, from "god-seeking" to "god-fighting" (i.e., theomachy).

Many people frankly build a name for themselves in the sport of "god-seeking." One recalls the stern condemnation of Bishop Michael (Gribanovsky) against all such "seeking." "They seek," he said, "because they have lost all principles; and while they look for better ones [principles], poorer ones take advantage of the confusion and cheat without any twinge of conscience: for what kind of conscience is there when no one knows what is true, what is good, what is evil."[104]

Intermediate understandings of religion and Christianity only estrange many people from the truth because, for one who sincerely seeks God, they become like "tollhouses." Many join the path of these arduous seekings, but very many do not complete it with success. A significant proportion remain "travelling from ordeal to ordeal," not finding blessed peace. Finally, in this realm of half-light, half-truth, in this realm of the lack of understanding and of the indefinite, in this "vague unsettled world," the very soul degenerates, becomes weak, and is poorly receptive to Grace-given inspiration. Such a soul will continue to seek even after it finds what it is looking for. Then there is created a pitiful type of "religious idler," as F. M. Dostoevsky called them.

The abovementioned state of affairs imposes a special responsibility on all Church members in our time. Members of the Church are very guilty in that they fail to point the way clearly and their examples poorly illuminate the final point of arrival for those who are seeking. This point is not the abstract understanding of Christianity, but precisely the Church of the living God.

According to the example of many people who have followed the agonizing path of seeking to its completion, it is possible to discern that a lasting peace draws near only when man comes to believe in the Church; when he accepts, with all his being, the idea of the Church in such a way that, for him, the separation of Christianity from the Church is inconceivable. Then begins the real quickening of Church life. Man feels that he is a branch of a great, ever-budding tree of the Church. He is conscious of himself not as a follower of some kind of school, but as a member of the body of Christ with whom he has a common life and from whom he receives this life.

Only one who has come to believe in the Church, who is guided by the concept of the Church in the appraisal of the phenomena of life and the direction of his personal life, who has felt Church life within himself, he and only he is on the correct path. Much that earlier seemed indefinite and vague will become obvious and clear. It is especially precious that in times of general vacillation, of wandering from side to side, from the right to the left and from the left to the right, every Church-conscious person feels himself standing on a steadfast, centuries-old rock that feels firm under his feet.

The Spirit of God lives in the Church. This is not a dry and dogmatic thesis, preserved only through respect for what is old. No, this is truth; truth which can be experienced and known by everyone who has been penetrated by Church consciousness. This Grace-filled Church life cannot be the subject of dry scholastic research, for it is accessible for study only through experience. Human language is capable of speaking only vaguely and unclearly about this Grace-filled life.

Saint Hilary of Poitiers spoke correctly when he said, "This is the characteristic virtue of the Church—that it becomes comprehensible when you adopt it."[105] Only he who has Church life knows about Church life, he requires no proofs; but for one who does not have it, it is something which cannot be proved.

For a member of the Church, the object of all his life must be constantly to unite more and more with the life of the Church, and, at the same time, to preach about the Church to others, not substituting it with Christianity, not substituting life with a dry and abstract teaching.

Now, there is too often talk about the insufficiency of life in the Church, about the "reviving" of the Church. All such talk is difficult to understand and we are very much inclined to acknowledge it as completely senseless. Life in the Church can never run low, for the Holy Spirit abides in it until the end of time (cf. John 14:16 ["I will pray the Father, and He will give you another Helper (the Holy Spirit), that He may abide with you forever"]).

There is life in the Church and only churchless people do not notice this life. The life of the Spirit of God is incomprehensible to a person who perceives solely with his mind; it may even seem foolish to him, for it is accessible only to a person who perceives with his spirit. People who are of an emotional mode of thinking seldom receive a feeling of the Church-conscious life; yet even now there are people, simple in heart and pious in life, who constantly live by this feeling of the abundant, Grace-filled life in the Church. This atmosphere of Church life and Church inspiration can especially be felt in monasteries.

Those who speak about the insufficiency of life in the Church usually refer to the insufficiencies of church administration, the thousands of consistorial papers, and so on. For all those who genuinely understand Church life, however, it is as clear as God's day that all these consistories with their ukases [proclamations] do not affect the depth of Church life at all. The deep river of abundant, Grace-filled life flows increasingly and gives drink to everyone who wishes to quench his spiritual thirst. This river cannot be dammed up with "paper."

No, it is not the insufficiency of life in the Church which must be spoken of, but of the insufficiency of

Church consciousness in us. Many live a Churchly life, not even clearly realizing the fact. Even if we consciously live a Churchly life, we preach little about the blessings of this life. With outsiders we usually only debate about Christian truths, forgetting about Church life. We also are sometimes capable of substituting the Church with Christianity, life with abstract theory.

Unfortunately, we ourselves do not value our Church and the great blessing of Church life enough. We do not confess our faith in the Church bravely, clearly, and definitely. While believing in the Church, we constantly seem to pardon ourselves for the fact that we still believe in it. We read the ninth article of the Creed "In one Holy, Catholic, and Apostolic Church …"] without any special joy, or even with a feeling of guilt.

A Church-conscious person is now often confronted with the exclamation of Turgenev's poetry in prose: "You still believe? But you are altogether a backward person!" And how many have so much courage as to bravely confess: "Yes, I believe in the One, Holy, Catholic and Apostolic Church, I belong to the Holy Orthodox Church and thus I am the most advanced person, for only in the Church is it possible to have that new life, for the sake of which the Son of God came to the sinful earth; only in the Church can one come to a measure of full growth in Christ—consequently, only in the Church is genuine progress possible!"

Are we not more often inclined to reply to the question "Are you not one of Christ's disciples?" with the answer "I do not know Him" (cf. John 18:25)?

Thus it must be considered as the most vital necessity of the present time to confess openly the indisputable truth that Christ created precisely the Church and that it is absurd to separate Christianity from the Church and absurd to speak of some sort of Christianity apart from the Holy Orthodox Church of Christ.

This truth, we believe, will illuminate, for many, the final goal in their wearisome journey of seeking; it will show them, not in lifeless teaching, but in Church life, where they can truly recover themselves out of the snare of the devil, who are taken captive by him at his will (cf. 2 Tim 2:26). This truth will also help us to identify Church life and to "gather the separated" children of the Church, so that all may be one, as the Lord Jesus Christ prayed before His sufferings.

We shall end our discourse with one parable of the type used by the holy Fathers. The Church is like a strong oak, and a man outside the Church is like a flying bird. See how the unfortunate bird struggles in a strong wind. How uneven is its flight! It either flies upward, or else it is overturned by the wind, or it moves slightly forward, and then it is again pushed backward. That is how a person is carried by the winds of false teaching. But just as the bird is calmed in the dense branches of the tree and peacefully looks out of its refuge on the storm raging past, so a man finds peace when he runs to the Church. From his calm refuge he looks out at the ferocious storm "near the Church walls" and he sorrows for the unfortunate people who are overtaken by this tempest outside the Church and who delay in seeking shelter under its abundant Grace, and he prays to the Lord: "Unite them to Thy Holy, Catholic, and Apostolic Church…, that they also may glorify with us the most honorable and majestic name of God praised in the Holy Trinity."

POINTS OF REFLECTION

1. Why was the teaching of Arius rejected by the Church?

2. The Orthodox Church teaches us that Jesus Christ is fully man and fully God. Why is this important to the understanding of salvation?

3. Christ said: "I also say to you that you are Peter, and on this rock I will build My church, and the gates of Hades shall not prevail against it" (Matt 16:18). As the Church is of Divine origin, why do some people see Christianity, or a Christian life, as possible without it?

4. Respect for Christianity can coexist with disdain for the Church or "organized religion." Why is this?

5. How can we communicate the work of the Holy Spirit within the Church to those outside of it who view it simply as a failed human institution?

6. What must we do to fully experience the life of the Church as Christ prayed for it to be?

A Biography
of Archbishop Ilarion (Troitsky)

The future Saint Ilarion was born on September 13, 1886, to the Troitsky family in Lipitsy, Kashira District, Tula Province, and named Vladimir. Both his grandfather Peter and his father Alexey were priests of the village of Lipitsy. Vladimir had two brothers and two sisters. After the death of their mother, the children were raised by her unmarried sister who was a parish school teacher. One brother became Bishop Daniel of Bryansk and the other, the youngest brother, was ordained and succeeded his father as priest in Lipitsy.

Vladimir Alexeyevich Troitsky felt the calling of a scholar within himself in the days of his earliest youth. As a seven-year-old boy, he took his three-year-old brother by the hand and led him from his native village to the town to study. When the younger one began to weep, he said, "Well then, remain uneducated…" Vladimir studied at the local church school in Tula, He graduated from the Tula Theological School in 1906 and entered the Moscow Theological Academy. He graduated with a degree in Theology from the academy in 1910 and received his Master's Degree from the same university in 1913. In March of that year, he was tonsured a monk at Holy Trinity Saint Sergius Monastery and given the name Ilarion. In May he was appointed inspector at the academy. In June he was ordained to the priesthood and in July he was raised to the rank of archimandrite and in December of the same year was appointed professor of Holy Scripture.

A prominent theologian and preacher, his entire life was an unquenchable flame of the greatest love for Christ's Church. His labors were characterized by a Church consciousness, a constant struggle against scholasticism and the Latinizations that penetrated theology from the time of Metropolitan Peter Mohila. In theological learning, his ideal was Churchliness and spirituality as opposed to scholastic and rationalism. His constant theme was that outside of the Church there is no salvation, outside the Church there are no sacraments.

This description was given of his personality and character: "Archbishop Ilarion, being a young man, enjoyed life from every aspect. He was educated, a beautiful orator, church preacher and singer, a brilliant polemicist against the godless, always natural, sincere, and open. Everywhere he went people were attracted to him and he was loved by all. Large in stature, with a broad chest, luxurious blond hair and a clear, bright face, he remains fixed in the memory of all those who have met him."

The Russian Patriarchate was dissolved by Tsar Peter the First in the 1700s. Archimandrite Ilarion made it clear that he was in favor of its restoration during the Local Council of 1917–1918. Here are the salient points regarding the issue from his reply (which appeared in *The Theological Herald*, January 1917) to a letter from Robert Gardiner, the secretary of the commission for the organization of a world conference of Christianity:

> The Russian Church has never been without a chief hierarch. Our Patriarchate was destroyed by Peter I. With whom did it interfere? With the conciliarity of the Church? But wasn't it during the time of the Patriarchs that there were especially many councils? No, the Patriarchate interfered neither with conciliarity nor with the Church. Then with whom? Here before me are two great friends, two adornments of the seventeenth century—Patriarch Nikon and Tsar Alexei Mikhailovich. In order to sow disagreement between these two friends, evil boyars whispered to the Tsar, "Because of the Patriarch, you, the Sovereign, have become invisible." When Nikon left the Moscow throne, he wrote, "Let the sovereign have more space without me." Peter gave flesh to this thought of Nikon's when he destroyed the Patriarchate. "Let me, the Sovereign, have more space without the Patriarch …"
>
> But Church consciousness, in the thirty-fourth Apostolic Canon, as well as in the Local Council held in Moscow in 1917, says one irrevocable thing: "The bishops of

any nation, including the Russian nation, must know who is the first among them, and acknowledge him as their head."

And I would like to address all those who for some reason still consider it necessary to protest against the Patriarchate. Fathers and brothers! Do not disrupt the joy of our oneness of mind! Why do you take this thankless task upon yourselves? Why do you make hopeless speeches? You are fighting against the Church's consciousness. Have some fear, lest haply you begin to fight against God (cf. Acts 5:39)! We have already sinned—sinned in that we didn't restore the Patriarchate two months ago, when we all came to Moscow and met with each other for the first time in the great Dormition Cathedral. Was it not painful to the point of tears to see the empty Patriarchal seat?... And when we venerated the holy relics of the wonderworkers of Moscow and chief hierarchs of Russia, did we not hear their reproach, that for two hundred years their chief hierarchical throne has remained desolate?"[106]

The Bolsheviks, a revolutionary far-left party led by Vladimir Lenin, came to power in 1917. The Russian Orthodox Church reestablished the patriarchate and elected Metropolitan Tikhon of Moscow as patriarch. Archimandrite Ilarion was one of the first supporters of the new patriarch and quickly met with the ire of the Bolshevik authorities. He was arrested and sent into exile for three months. He was ordained to the episcopacy in

May of 1920 becoming the Bishop of Verey, a vicariate in the Moscow diocese and found himself at the center of the Church's administration as Patriarch Tikhon's intimate counselor and vicar bishop. Bishop Ilarion was a most eloquent preacher and all the faithful of Moscow flocked to hear him. He spent one year in exile in the city of ArchangeIsk. On his return, he was raised to the rank of archbishop.

Archbishop Ilarion selflessly struggled against atheism and schism, dealing heavy blows to both atheists and renovationists. He tirelessly preached against them in churches, carried out brilliant public debates with the representatives of one and the other, organized the denial of the church buildings to the renovators, testified to the truth in interrogations in prison even under heavy threats when so many in like situations had fallen. When conversation touched upon the relationship between the authorities and the church administration, he would say, "One must actually be in this situation, if only a little, otherwise it is impossible to describe it. This is Satan himself."

In December 1923, the Bolsheviks sent Archbishop Ilarion to the Solovsky prison camp (formerly the Solovetsky Monastery) for three years. Arriving a week before the Feast of the Nativity of Christ and seeing the horror of the situation and the camp food, even he, brave and full of the love of life, said, "We will never leave here alive."

One of his fellow inmates wrote:

During our years of imprisonment, we were all witnesses to his completely monastic characteristics: non-acquisitiveness, profound simplicity, genuine humility, and childlike meekness. He had no interest in his possessions and he simply gave away whatever anyone asked for. Someone even had to look after his suitcase for him; fortunately, he had a postulant at Solovky who took care of this matter. His captivating spirit of non-acquisitiveness was truly after the manner of Metropolitan Antony [Khrapovitsky], whose school many praised.

One could insult Vladyka Ilarion but he would never make a reply, perhaps he would never even notice it. He was always jolly and even when he was pre-occupied or agitated, he would quickly try to cover this with that same jolliness. He looked at everything with spiritual eyes and everything served him for the strengthening of his spirit.

On the Filomonov wharf, seven versts from the Solovetsky citadel and the main camp, on the shore of the small bay of the White Sea, Archbishop Ilarlon, two other bishops, several priests and we, all prisoners, were occupied as net-weavers and fishermen. Archbishop Ilarion liked to describe this work of ours by paraphrasing the words of the sticheron for Pentecost: "The Holy Spirit provides every gift: before, the fishermen became theologians, but now it is reversed—the theologians become fishermen." Thus did his spirit become reconciled with the new situation.

His gentleness extended even to the Soviet power itself and he could look upon it without guile. The Soviets had given all of us churchmen equal lengths of imprisonment so that Archbishop Ilarion, who had toiled near the Patriarch in Moscow and who had dealt heavy blows to atheism and to the renovationists, being a giant in the general Russian measure, and a young hieromonk from Kazan whose only crime consisted in removing the stole from a renovationist deacon and not allowing the latter to serve with him, were both sentenced to three years.

"Gracious is this master," Archbishop Ilarion used to say in this regard with the words of John Chrysostom, "to welcome the last one just as the first one; to accept the one who had toiled from the first hour, and welcome his deeds and accept his intentions and honor his acts and praise his deeds…" These words rang ironically, but gave us the feeling of peace and caused us to accept the trial as being from God's hand.

This meekness was not, however, a loss of courage in the face of the God-hating power. While still at the Kemsk camp at the gates of Solovky, Lenin's death was announced to us. We were instructed to stand in silence for five minutes at the time his body would be lowered into the grave in Moscow. Vladyka Ilarion and I were lying on the plank beds while our fathers and brethren of various ranks stood in a line opposite us in the center of the barracks in anticipation of the "solemn" moment. They urged us "Get up; he is a great man anyway and besides, we will be in trouble if they notice." Looking at Vladyka, I too did not rise. There was still enough strength left not to bow our heads to this beast. Thus, we did not rise and so harm befell us. Vladyka said, "Think, fathers, of what is happening in hell today. Lenin himself has arrived there; it is such a triumph for the demons."

Vladyka Ilarion was overjoyed by the idea that Solovky was a school of virtue—non acquisitiveness, meekness, humility, restraint, patience, and love of toil. A group of clergy which had just arrived was robbed and the fathers were very grieved. When I jokingly said to them that in this way they were being taught non-acquisitiveness, Vladika was in ecstasy. Twice in a row I had my boots stolen and I strolled about the camp in torn galoshes, an act which would bring Vladyka that sort of pleasure with which he taught us to rejoice in meekness. It is necessary to note, however, that not all aesthetically minded monks understood such a spirit. It seemed to some that advance in spiritual struggles is only in monastic surroundings so at times they were deeply grieved by their deprivation.

Archbishop Ilarion's love towards every man, his interest in each one and his sociability were simply extraordinary. He was the most popular figure in camp amongst all of us and even though there were more senior bishops, and no less educated than he; the general, the officer, the student and professor: they knew him and conversed with him. The brigands, the grave criminal offenders, the criminal world thought of him as a good, respected man one could not help but like.

At moments of rest or in free hours, he could be seen strolling arm in arm with many such specimens from this criminal class. This was not condescension towards a younger brother or a fallen man. No, Vladyka conversed with each one and was equally interested in the "profession" or any matter which interested each person. The brigand is very proud and sensitive: One cannot show them contempt with impunity. His manner was all-conquering, he, as a friend, he ennobled them with his presence and attention. It was of singular interest to observe him in his element sharing with them. He was approachable to all, he was liked by everybody. It was easy for everyone to be with him, to meet with him, and come to him. Vladyka himself had a most common, simple exterior, but behind this joviality and common appeal one could gradually discern a child-like purity, his great spiritual experience, goodness, compassion, a delightful Indifference to wealth, sincere faith, genuine piety, a high moral perfection, a strong mind with clear convictions. This exterior of foolishness and mask of common worldliness hid his inner life from people and saved him from developing hypocrisy or conceit. He was completely opposed to all hypocrisy and false piety. In the "Troitsky Work Group," as Archbishop Ilarion's crew was called, the clergy received a good education on the Solovky school of virtues.

Everyone learned that to calI oneself a sinner and to carry on Iong pious conversations, and to demonstrate the severity of one's life gives no benefit to others and only leads one to become conceited. Vladika would naturally ask each arriving priest for a list of everything that preceded his imprisonment.

"What were you arrested for?"

"Well, I used to serve thanksgiving prayers at home after they closed the monastery," replied one abbot, "People would gather and there were even healings…"

"Ah, is that so, there were even healings. And how much time at Solovky did they give you?"

"Three years."

"Well that is not much, for healings, they should have given you more. The Soviet authorities did not investigate carefully enough…"

It is readily understandable that to speak of healing as a result of one's own prayers was more than immodest.

At the end of summer, 1925, Archbishop Ilarion was suddenly transferred from the Solovetsky camp to the Yaroslav prison. In the Spring of 1926, he was with us again. . . .

In the Yaroslav prison, Vladika was given great favors. He could receive books and he read much literature of the holy Fathers and wrote several thick notebooks which he was allowed to hand over to his friends for preservation (after prison censorship). He would secretly visit the quarters of the prison supervisor, a good person, and there he saw a collection of contemporary handwritten underground religious literature and copies of eleven kinds of church administrative documents and the correspondence of hierarchs. Vladyka remembered his stay in Yaroslav prison as the best time of his imprisonment, in spite of the unpleasantness with the enemy of the Church.

In June of 1927, he was transferred to Moscow to meet with secular persons and with Archbishop Gregory who hoped to convince him to head the Gregorian Supreme Church Council. He refused and was sent back to Solovsky.

In 1929 the Bolsheviks decided to send Archbishop Ilarion to Alma-Ata in Central Asia. He was to be sent by stages, from one deportation prison to the other. He was robbed on the road and arrived in Petersburg in rags, swarming with parasites, and already ill. From the Petrograd prison hospital in which he had been placed, he wrote: "I am seriously ill with spotted typhus; I am lying in a prison hospital. I must have become infected on the road. On Saturday, December 15/28, my fate will be decided (the crisis of the illness); it is doubtful if I will survive."

On December 15/28, 1929, he was informed in the hospital that he had to be shaved. He said, "Do with me now what you wish." In delirium he said, "And now I am altogether free; no one will take me." He died that day.

At night the body of Archbishop Ilarion was placed in a hastily made coffin of rough boards, and given to his nearest relatives for burial. Always noted for his tallness and robust health, when the coffin was opened, exile had so changed Vladyka that no one recognized him. In the coffin lay a pitiful, shaven, gray old man. One of the female relatives fainted. Metropolitan Seraphim (Chichagov) brought his own white vestments and a white miter, and after Vladyka's body was vested in these it was placed in a better coffin. The funeral service was celebrated by Metropolitan Seraphim himself, co-served by six hierarchs and a multitude of clergy, and a choir sang. Vladyka Ilarion was buried in the Novodevichy Monastery cemetery.

Thus this giant in spirit and body, this man of such a marvelous soul, endowed by the Lord with eminent theological gifts, departed into eternity. He gave his life for Christ's Church.[107]

Hieromartyr Ilarion, Archbishop of Verey, was glorified as a saint on May 10, 1999, by the Russian Orthodox Church and his relics were transferred to the Sretensky Monastery in Moscow.

Notes

Part I: The Unity of Believers

1   "Ascetic Regulations" (in Russian), Chap. 18, *Works*, Part 5, 4th ed., pp. 359, 360, Trinity-Saint Sergius Lavra, 1902.

2   "Letter 62" (in Russian), *Works,* 2nd ed., Part 1, pp. 363–364, Kiev, 1891.

3   "On the Lord's Prayer" (in Russian), *Works,* Part 2, pp. 221, 217.

4   "Interpretation of the Evangelist John" (in Russian), Book 2, Chap. 2, *Works,* Moscow Eccl. Acad. Edition, Part 15, pp. 105–112 passim. Cf. "Moral Concept of the Dogma of the Church" (in Russian), by Archbishop Anthony (Khrapovitsky), *Collection,* 2nd ed., Vol. 2, St Petersburg, 1911; and "Moral Concept of the Dogma of the All-Holy Trinity" (in Russian), ibid., pp. 70–76.

5   *Prayer Book*, 4th ed. revised (Jordanville, NY: Holy Trinity Monastery, 2005), p. 217.

6   *Justification of the Good*, 2nd ed. (in Russian), p. 462, 1899.

7   *Prayer Book*, p. 217 [Kontakion for Pentecost Sunday].

8   Cf. 1 Cor 6:15; 10:17; 12:13, 27; Eph 1:23; 4:4, 12, 16, 25; 5:23, 30; Col 1:18, 24; 2:19; 3:15.

9   "On the Epistle to the Ephesians" (in Russian), Homily 9, *Works*, St Petersburg Eccl. Acad. Edition, Vol. 2, p. 86.

10   Ibid., p. 96.

11   *Works,* Part 7, p. 434, Moscow, 1861.

12   *Works,* Kiev Eccl. Acad. Edition, book 17, p. 297.

13 *Interpretation of the Epis.,* p. 123, Kazan, 1867.

14 *Works,* Part 7, p. 134.

15 "On the Epistle to the Ephesians," Homily 2, *Works,* Vol. 2, p. 96.

16 For a detailed interpretation of this verse, see Prof. D. J. Bogdashevsky, *On the Epistle of the Holy Apostle Paul to the Ephesians* (in Russian), pp. 557–565, Kiev, 1904; see also Ivan Mansvetov, *The New Testament Teaching of the Church* (in Russian), pp. 143–160, Moscow, 1879.

17 "He depicted his thoughts rather unclearly because he wished to express everything at once" says St John Chrysostom ("On the Epistle to the Ephesians," Hom. 11, *Works,* Vol. 11, p. 100.).

18 Ibid., pp. 100–101.

19 *Works,* Part 7, p. 438.

20 *Opera,* Vol. 2, pp. 187 B-C, 180 D, Le Quien, Paris, 1712.

21 *Interpretation of the Epistle to the Ephesians* (in Russian), p. 132, Kazan, 1881.

22 *Interpretation of the Epistle of the Apostle Paul to the Ephesians* (in Russian), p. 307, 2nd edition, Moscow, 1883.

23 St John Chrysostom, ibid., p. 101.

24 St Cyprian of Carthage, "On the Unity of the Church," Chap. 23, *Works,* Part 2, p. 197.

25 Ibid., Chap. 5, *Works,* Part 2, p. 180.

26 Regarding the word "Christianity" and similar words with the *cmeo* (pronounced: *stvo*) ending in Russian. No such words exist in the original Greek text although some Protestant translations insert them arbitrarily.

27 Cf. Archbishop Anthony (Khrapovitsky), Collection, 2nd ed., Vol. 2, p. 16, St Petersburg, 1911.

28 "Der Beweis des Glaubens," S 585, 1875.

29 *The Church Formation in the First Centuries of Christianity* (in Russian), Trans. of A. Petrovsky and P. Florensky, 1906.

30   "On the Unity of the Catholic Church," Chap. 14, *Works*, Part 2, pp. 188–189.

31   "Letter 43, to Antonianus," *Works*, Part 1, p. 236; "Letter to Stephen," ibid., p. 330.

32   "Letter 62, to Magnus," ibid., p. 360.

33   [Novatian was a third-century bishop whose followers formed a schismatic group. He took the position that those who denied their Christian faith when under persecution had to be re-baptized in order to come back to the Church.—Ed.]

34   "Letter 55, to Stephen," ibid., p. 312.

35   "Letter 62, to Magnus," ibid., p. 361.

36   "On the Unity of the Catholic Church," Chap. 15, *Works*, Part 2, p. 190. Cf. "On the Lord's Prayer," Chap. 24, ibid., pp. 217–218; "Letter 43, to Antonianus," *Works*, Part 1, p. 239.

37   "Letter 62, to Magnus," ibid., p. 371.

38   "Letter 58, to Quintus," ibid., pp. 326–327.

39   "Letter 61, to Pompei," ibid., p. 353; "Letter 57, to Januarius," ibid., p. 326.

40   "Letter 56, to Quintus," ibid., p. 326; "On the Unity of the Church," p. 197.

41   "On the Unity of the Church," Chap. 4, *Works*, Part 2, pp. 179–180.

42   Ibid., p. 178.

43   Ibid., p. 189.

44   Ibid., pp. 190–192; cf. "Letter 60, to Jubaian," p. 334.

45   "Letter 60, to Jubaian," Works, Part 1, pp. 334–335.

46   "Letter 40, to Cornelius," ibid., p. 205.

47   "Letter 62, to Magnus," ibid., pp. 360–361, citing Luke 11:23, Matt 18:17. Cf. "Letter 57, to Januarius," pp. 324–325; "Letter 61, to Pompei," p. 351.

48   "Letter 43," ibid., p. 212.

49   "Letter 42, to Cornelius," ibid., p. 212.

50 "Habere iam non potest Eeum patrum, qui Ecclesiam non habet matrem"; "On the Unity of the Church," Chap. 6, *Works,* Part 2, p. 181. Cf. Chap. 17, p. 191. "Can it be imagined that one who acts against Christ's priests, separates himself from intercourse with His clergy and people, is found to be with Christ?"

51 "Letter 58, to Quintas," Chap. 1, *Works,* Part 1, p. 325.

52 Ibid., p. 326.

53 "On the Unity of the Church," Chap. 11, *Works,* Part 2, pp. 185–186. Cf. "Letter 60, to Jubaian," ibid., Part 1, p. 346.

54 Migne, P. L., t. 3, Coll. 1077–1078.

55 Cf. Mark 1:24; Luke 8:28. Contra litteral Petiliani III, 34, 39. Migne, P. L., t. 43, col. 460.

56 Contra Cresconium, I, 22, 27. Migne, P. L., t. 43, col. 460.

57 De baptismo, I 7, 9, Migne, P. L., t. 43, col. 115.

58 Contra Cresconium, I, 29, 34. Migne, P. L., t. 43, col. 463–464.

59 The Donatist schism evolved in North Africa in the fourth century at the end of the persecution of Diocletian. Some clergy who had renounced their faith wanted to return to the Church. Donatus and his followers allowed that they may return as laymen but not as clergy. They also opposed Bishop Caecilian as had been ordained by the bishop who lapsed and Caecilian was willing to allow repentant clergy to return to office.

60 De baptismo, I, 2, 3. Migne, P. L., t. 43, col. 110. Contra Cresconium, ibid., col. 460, 563.

61 Cf. 1 Cor 13:1–3. In I Ioan. tract. 5, 6. Migne, P. L., t. 35, col. 2015.

62 De baptismo, I, 9, 12. Migne, P. L., t. 43, col. 116.

63 Ibid.

64 De baptismo, I, 10, 14. Migne, P. L., t. 43, col. 117–118.

65 De baptismo, I, 12, 18. Migne, P. L., t. 43, col. 119.

66 De baptismo, I, 12, 20; I, 13, 21. Migne, P. L., t. 43, col. 119, 120, 121.

67 De baptismo, I, 15, 23. Migne, P. L., t. 43, col. 121.

68 Contra Cresconium, II, 14, 17. Migne, P. L., t. 43, col. 477.

69 De baptismo, III, 16, 21. Migne, P. L., t. 43, col. 148.

70 Epistle 61, 2. Migne, P. L., t. 33, col. 229.

71 Contra litteras Petiliani, II 77, 172. De baptismo, IV, 17, 24. Migne, P. L., t. 43, col. 312, 169.

72 Epistle 185, 10, 46. Migne, P. L., t. 33, col. 813.

73 Contra epistles Parmeniani, II, 11, 25. Migne, P. L., t. 43, col. 69.

74 Sermon 268, 2. Migne, P. L., t. 38, col. 1232, Contra Cresconium, II, 12, 15; II. 13, 16; II, 14, 17. Migne, P. L., t. 43, col. 476, 477.

75 Epistle 185, 9, 42. Migne, P. L., t. 33, col. 811.

76 Epistle 208, 6. Epistle 185, 9, 42. Migne, P. L., t. 33, col. 952, 811. Contra epist. Parmeniani, II, 3, 6. Migne, P. L., t 43, col. 54.

77 Quaest. in eptat. 5, 15. Migne, P. L., t. 34, col. 755.

78 Contra litteras Petiliani, II, 77, 172. Migne, P. L., t. 43, col. 312.

79 De baptismo, III, 16, 21. Migne, P. L., t. 43, col. 148.

80 Ad Roman, III, 3.

Part II: The Place of the Church

81 The Nicene Creed: *The Divine Liturgy of Our Father Among the Saints Basil the Great: Slavonic-English Parallel* (Jordanville, New York: Holy Trinity Publications, 2020) p. 164–165.

82 *Paternal Testament* (in Russian), publication edited by E. M. Prilezhaev, pp. 3, 6, St Petersburg, 1893.

83 *Reminder* (in Russian), I, Chap. 25, 26, Translation of Reader P. Ponomarev, pp. 44, 48, Kazan, 1904.

84 *Against Heresies*, book 3, Chap. 1 §1.

85 See the introduction (forward) to the Geneva edition of a "summary of the Gospel."

86   See Prof. A. A. Spassky, "The History of the Dogmatic Movement in the Epoch of the Ecumenical Councils" (in Russian), p. 651, Sergiev Posad, 1906.

87   Ibid.

88   St Athanasius, *On the Incarnation*, 54:3 [John Behr, *On the Incarnation: Saint Athanasius The Great of Alexandria* (London: SPCK, 2011).].

89   Saint Irenaeus of Lyons, *Against Heresies*, III.19.1 [Alexander Roberts and William Rambaut, Trans. Ante-Nicene Fathers, Vol. 1. (Buffalo, NY: Christian Literature Publishing Co., 1885).].

90   See Prof. J. V. Popov, "The Idea of Deification in the Ancient Eastern Church" (in Russian), Moscow, 1909. Also see his "Religious Ideal of St Athanasius of Alexandria" (in Russian), Holy Trinity St Sergius Lavra, 1904. Cf. Prof. Spassky, ibid., pp. 198, 199.

91   *The Services of Christmas* (Syosset, NY: Department of Religious Education/OCA, 1981), pp. 72–73.

92   Ibid., p. 76.

93   Ibid., pp. 88–89.

94   *Proofs from the Apostolic Sermons*, Chap. 99 [J. Armitage Robinson, trans. *The Proof of the Apostolic Preaching* (London, 1920) https://www.tertullian.org/fathers/irenaeus_02_proof.htm].

95   *Against Heresies*, Book 4, Chap. 34 §1.

96   David Friedrich Strauss (1808–1874) was a German Protestant theologian who wrote on the historical Jesus.

97   The Russian author Leo Tolstoy (1828–1910) was told by his older brother that there was a green stick buried in the forest with words carved it that would bring peace to all and do away with death.

98   Wilhelm Hohoff, *Die Revolution seit dem Sechszenten Jahrhunrt*, s. 150, Frieburg im reisgau, 1887.

99 Ferdinand Kattenbusch, *Von Schleiermacher zu Ritschl,* s. 5, Griessen, 1893.

100 *Der Katholik,* Bd. 2, ss. 400–401, 1889.

101 Terentiev, *The Lutheran Denominational System according to the Symbolic Books of Lutheranism* (in Russian), p. 460, Kazan, 1910.

102 See *Compositions,* vol. 2, first letter to Palmer ["Unia" is the name given to various attempts in the past thousand years to reunite groups of Orthodox believers to the Roman Catholic Church whereby the former are permitted to retain their original liturgical and pastoral practices as long as they acknowledge the Roman Catholic Bishop of Rome as the head of the Universal Church.—Ed.].

103 *Vekhi (Guideposts)* was a journal of the late nineteenth century which commented on the social, spiritual, and moral crises in Russia and advocated a return to the true Russian faith and traditions.—Trans.

104 *Letters of the late Michael, Bishop of Tavra* (in Russian), Simferopol, 1910, p. 178.

105 De Trinitate, VIII, 4.

Appendix

106 Translated by Nun Corneilia, see https://orthochristian.com/33316.html

107 This text is based on the article: Michael Polsky, "The Holy New Martyr Archbishop Ilarion," *Orthodox Life*, Issue 3, 1971, p. 10. The *Orthodox Life* article was a translation from *New Martyrs of Russia, Vol. I,* compiled by Protopresbyter Michael Polsky (Jordanville, NY: Holy Trinity Monastery, 1949), pp. 125, 134.

Scripture Index

Subject Index